Reading the Letters
of Saint Paul

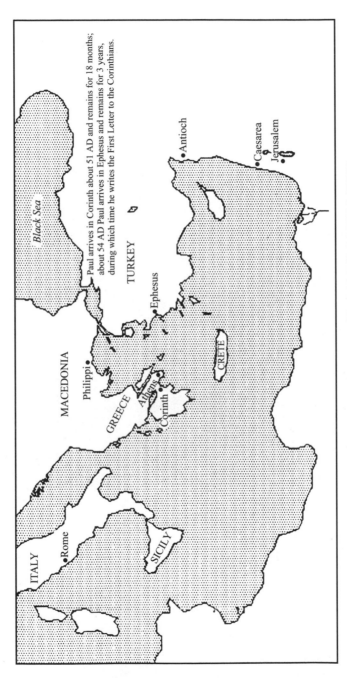

Paul arrives in Corinth about 51 AD and remains for 18 months; about 54 AD Paul arrives in Ephesus and remains for 3 years, during which time he writes the First Letter to the Corinthians.

MEDITERRANEAN SEA AND PAUL'S JOURNEYS

READING THE LETTERS OF SAINT PAUL

Study, Reflection and Prayer

CAROLYN THOMAS, S.C.N.

PAULIST PRESS
New York / Mahwah, N.J.

The Publisher gratefully acknowledges the use of the following: The English translation of the prayers for the feast of St.Vincent de Paul and for the Common of the Dedication of a Church from *The Roman Missal* © 1973, International Committee on English in the Liturgy, Inc. All rights reserved. The prayers from *New St. Joseph People's Prayer Book* (copyright © 1993, 1980) are reproduced with permission from Catholic Book Publishing Co., New York, N.Y.: "For a Happy Death," "To Encounter God Frequently in Prayer," "On Finding God after a Long Search," "Self-Offering to the Trinity," "To Be a True Servant of God," "Anima Christi," "For a Holy Death," "To Pray Always," "For the Gift to Seek God," "To Be Clothed with All the Virtues," "To End Discord," "For All Church Leaders," "To Practice What Jesus Taught," "Praise and Petition," "To Remain Steadfast in the Faith," "For the Grace to Help Others." "For Christ's Mercy," "For the Conversion of Unbelievers," "To Work for the Things We Pray For," "Gratitude for God's Goodness to Us Sinners," "Self-Offering to God," "To Do God's Will," "For a Strong Virtue of Hope." All rights reserved. "Prayer of St. Augustine," EWTN.com. Used with permission. "Prayer of Transformation, " "The Christopher Prayer," Warren Dicharry, *To Live the Word Inspired and Incarnate*, 1985. Alba House, New York, N.Y. Used with permission. All rights reserved. New Testament citations are from the Revised Standard Version of the Bible, copyright 2nd edition, 1971 by the Division of Christian Education of the National Council of the Churches of Christ in the United States of America. Used with permission. All rights reserved. The Old Testament citations are from the New American Bible, unless otherwise indicated. Copyright © 1970 by the Confraternity of Christian Doctrine, Washington, D.C. Used with permission. All right reserved.

Cover design by Valerie Petro

Text design by Joseph E. Petta

Copyright © 2002 by Carolyn Thomas

Library of Congress Cataloging-in-Publication Data

Thomas, Carolyn, 1936–
   Reading the letters of St. Paul : study, reflection and prayer / by Carolyn Thomas.
      p.   cm.
   Includes bibliographical references and index.
   ISBN 0-8091-4065-9 (alk. paper)
      1. Bible. N.T. Epistles of Paul—Textbooks. 2. Bible. N.T. Epistles of Paul—Devotional literature.
I. Title.

BS2650.55 .T48 2002
227'.06—dc21

                                                                                        2001058765

Published by Paulist Press
997 Macarthur Boulevard
Mahwah, New Jersey 07430

www.paulistpress.com

Printed and bound in the
United States of America

Contents

To all my friends,
especially
Helen and Andy Chavez,
and
Kathy Gaiser

Introduction

*W*hy would anyone in the twenty-first century want to read a book on the teachings of St. Paul as found in letters written a couple of centuries ago? Was he not a man who started Christian communities in an era when people were not so busy and who lacked technical entertainment that we enjoy today? Moreover, the needs of first-century Christians differed from those of the modern Christian. His letters seem to be directed to a particular group of people, and sometimes, in instructing them, we get the picture of a man who confused and angered people of his own day, to say nothing of many others of our contemporary society.

Such are the questions and observations that will be addressed in the unfolding of this book's pages which are aimed at casting light on Paul's teachings as they come to us in his letters. In deciphering some of Paul's messages, we will explore how meaningful they are for life today in light of their significance for the lives of the first-century converts to Christianity.

We may consider ourselves to be very different and set apart from the first-century Christians, not only by cultural differences and the span of two centuries, but also by distinct needs, interests and varied goals. My hope is to bring the reader to see how the missives of St. Paul, couched in first-century letters and inspired by the Holy Spirit, are not only relevant for us today, but have the power to bring us to a new or renewed fervor, and to a more intimate relationship with God.

The following pages will provide some insights into the major issues covered in each of Paul's letters, as well as those attributed to Paul (i.e., the Post-Pauline Letters). Each chapter begins with a brief background of the church to which the letter is addressed. A short outline of the letter follows, which is to act as a "map" to give the reader an idea of what can be expected in the letter. Following the outline is an interpretation of three or more passages from each letter that are salient for understanding Paul's message for a particular church in the first century.

Following the interpretation of each passage, there are questions for reflection to assist the readers in the process of incorporating into their lives the divinely inspired message. The section then ends with a prayer related to the topic in the passage selected for interpretation. The prayers are taken from the church's rich tradition of prayers, mostly from the saints and the early church fathers, as well as a few prayers from more modern writers and from the church's Liturgy of the Hours.

After each chapter, there is a brief summary of major points that were considered in the interpretation, succeeded by a short bibliography for those who may wish to pursue further the study of St. Paul's letters. Given the content and organization of each chapter, the book may be used for: individual study; reflection and prayer; college courses on St. Paul's writings; study groups in a parish or neighborhood; or as a resource to homilists and all those who teach God's word.

First Letter
to the Thessalonians

INTRODUCTION

*T*he First Letter to the Thessalonians is the oldest Christian document that we have today. Paul probably wrote the letter around A.D. 50. Some of the contents of the letter give us the most ancient witness to the difficulties encountered by the early Christians between the death and resurrection of Jesus and the writings of the New Testament.

Thessalonica was an important political, commercial and economic city. It was located on the Egnatian Way, a major road that connected Rome and cities to the east. After the Romans captured Thessalonica in 168 B.C., they later made it the capital city of Macedonia. In 42 B.C., Thessalonica cooperated with the imperial army in the battle of Pydna, and Rome rewarded the city by making it a free city with its own seat of government. Archaeological findings point to a number of gods and goddesses, among whom were Anubis, Isis, Serapic and Osiris, who were venerated in Thessalonica.[1]

Paul, along with Silvanus and Timothy, went to Thessalonica about A.D. 50 on his second missionary journey after they were expelled from Philippi (Acts 16:16–40). The city had a Jewish synagogue, which gave Paul a forum for his preaching. He was so successful that some of the Jewish population succeeded in getting them expelled from Thessalonica as well. The Thessalonians were among Paul's first Greek converts, which accounts perhaps for the affection Paul shows for this church.

The question of the return of the Lord, or the *parousia,* is the most important topic Paul deals with in his letter to the Thessalonian Church. The first passage below reflects the faith life of the church at Thessalonica. The other two passages concern the major issues of interest among the Thessalonians, that is, the coming of the day of the Lord, its nature and time.

Outline of 1 Thessalonians

Greetings (1 Thess 1:1–2)

I. Gratitude for the Thessalonian Church
   (1 Thess 1:3–13)

II. Call to Holiness of Life (1 Thess 2:1–4:12)

III. Resurrection and the Lord's Coming
   (1 Thess 4:13–5:11)

Closing (5:12–28)

I. THE FAITH AND EXAMPLE
OF THE THESSALONIANS

Preparation: Read 1 Thessalonians 1:1 through 4:12. Paul expresses gratitude for the faith of the Thessalonians and exhorts them to live the Christian life as he taught them while he lived among them.

> We give thanks to God always for you all, constantly mentioning you in our prayers, remembering before

our God and Father your work of faith and labor of love and steadfastness of hope in our Lord Jesus Christ. For we know, beloved by God, that he has chosen you; for our gospel came to you not only in word, but also in power and in the Holy Spirit and with full conviction.... [Y]ou became imitators of us and of the Lord, for you received the word in much affliction, with joy inspired by the Holy Spirit; so that you became an example to all the believers in Macedonia and in Achaia.... [W]e were ready to share with you not only the gospel of God, but our own selves, because you had become very dear to us.... When you received the word of God which you heard from us, you accepted it not as the word of men, but...the word of God which is at work in you believers.... You...became imitators of the churches of God in Christ Jesus which are in Judea; for you suffered the same things from your own countrymen as they did.... This is the will of God, your sanctification: that you abstain from unchastity;...you yourselves have been taught by God to love one another.... We exhort you...to live quietly, to mind your own affairs, and to work with your hands, as we charged you. (1 Thess 1:2–4:12)

After Paul's greeting, he thanks God for the fidelity in the faith of his converts, and he continually remembers their good works of faith, which, Paul maintains, flow out of their faith and hope in Christ Jesus. For Paul, faith, love and hope are visible signs of the Thessalonians' spirituality. These virtues are the armor of Christians who live as foreigners in this world as long as they are away from their heavenly home. Thus Paul exhorts the Thessalonians to "put on the breastplate of faith and love, and for a helmet the hope of salvation" (1 Thess 5:8).

Paul spells out the meaning of faith, hope and love for the Thessalonian Church. The Thessalonians had already given evidence of their faith, which they expressed in action not only by their acceptance of the gospel but also by their evangelization of others: "For not only has the word of the Lord sounded forth from you in Macedonia and Achaia, but your faith in God has gone forth everywhere, so that we need not say anything" (1 Thess 1:8). Genuine Christian action is "faith working through love" (Gal 5:6).

Love, Paul points out, also expresses itself in action. The love of the Thessalonians was manifest in their remembrance of Paul, Silvanus and Timothy: "Timothy has come to us from you and has brought us the good news of your faith and love and reported that you always remember us kindly and long to see us, as we long to see you" (1 Thess 3:6). Paul states that he doesn't need to say a lot about love because the Thessalonians had been "taught by God to love one another" (1 Thess 4:9). One way in which they are to safeguard their charity or love is to live quietly without gossiping and keep themselves busy. Paul's own love had been demonstrated to them through sacrificial work out of devotion to Christ: "For you remember our labor and toil...; we worked night and day, that we might not burden any of you, while we preached to you the gospel of God" (1 Thess 2:9).

Hope, Paul goes on to explain, is the virtue by which a Christian trusts that God will continue to show loving care and that God will be there for and with the Christian as he or she suffers through the trials of this life in a world hostile to God. "For what is our hope or joy or crown of boasting before our Lord Jesus at his coming? Is it not you? For you are our glory and joy" (1 Thess 2:19–20).

Paul firmly believed that the conversion of the Thessalonians was the work of God. God's choice of them empowered Paul to take the gospel to them, "not only in word, but also in power and in the Holy Spirit and with full conviction" (1 Thess 1:5). Their acceptance of the gospel resulted in their being persecuted for their faith in Jesus Christ. In this, the Thessalonians, Paul says, imitated both him and Christ. Moreover, they had borne their afflictions with joy. In this, they "became an example to all the believers in Macedonia and Achaia" (1 Thess 1:7).

Persecution from unbelievers had not shaken the Thessalonians in their conviction of the gospel. For Paul, it was good news that they had been faithful witnesses and were holding steadfast to what they had been taught (1 Thess 2:14–16).

For Reflection

1. What is the most frequent content of your prayers?
2. Prayer of thanksgiving enables one to focus on God rather than exclusively on one's own needs and desires. What things are you particularly grateful for in your life?
3. What expressions of faith, hope and love are you aware of in your daily life? Have you ever experienced opposition to your faith in Christ?

Prayer to Encounter God Frequently in Prayer
Author Unknown

HEAVENLY FATHER,
    Let me realize that, like all prayer,
        prayer of petition is primarily a means of
          encountering you
        and being sustained by you.
    You know what we need because you are a loving
        Father
    who watches over us at every moment.
    Yet you respect our freedom
        and wait for us to express our needs to you.

Let me have frequent recourse to you in prayer
   so that I will purify my intentions
   and bring my wishes into conformity with your
      own.
Let me pray with fixed formulas
   as well as in my own words—whether they be long
      or short.
Above all, let me come before you with a heart moved
      by your Spirit
   and a will ready to conform to your holy will.[2]

II. THE COMING OF THE LORD

Preparation: Read 1 Thessalonians 4:13 through 4:18 (see below) in which St. Paul sets forth the basis for the Thessalonians' faith in the return of the Lord in glory and an apocalyptic[3] explanation of the coming.

But we would not have you ignorant…concerning those who are asleep, that you may not grieve as others do who have no hope. For since we believe that Jesus died and rose again, even so, through Jesus, God will bring with him those who have fallen asleep. For this we declare to you by the word of the Lord, that we who are alive, who are left until the coming of the Lord, shall not precede those who have fallen asleep. For the Lord himself will descend from heaven with a cry of command, with the archangel's call, and with the sound of the trumpet of God. And the dead in Christ will rise first; then we who are alive, who are left, shall be caught up together with them in the clouds to meet the Lord in the air; and so we shall always be with the Lord. Therefore comfort one another with these words. (1 Thess 4:13–18)

The concept of the *parousia* (that is, the day of the Lord) is introduced in the Old Testament. God would come to the world, and the Son of man would come to exercise power over the world and to judge it. Daniel's vision is described thus: "As the visions during the night continued, I saw/ One like a son of man coming,/ on the clouds of heaven;/ When he reached the Ancient One/ and was presented before him,/ He received dominion, glory and kingship;/ nations and peoples of every language serve him./ His dominion is an everlasting dominion/ that shall not be taken away,/ his kingship shall not be destroyed" (Dan 7:13–14; NAB).

The issue of the return of the Lord was introduced in the first chapter of the Letter to the Thessalonians in the context of Paul's affirmation of their faith. He commends them for turning to the true God "to wait for his Son from heaven, whom he raised from the dead, Jesus who delivers us from the wrath to come" (1 Thess 1:10). In this passage, Paul is responding to the Thessalonians' concern about those who have already died. Would they miss the joyous return of the Lord when he comes again?

Paul describes the Christians who have died as "those who have fallen asleep" (1 Thess 4:13). "To fall asleep" was a metaphor for dying among the early Christians. The expression stressed the idea of death having lost its permanency because of the death and resurrection of Jesus. While mental health experts today might call this a denial of reality, it was for the early Christians an expression of faith. Paul is concerned that the Thessalonians understand the nature of death for the baptized person and that they distinguish themselves from the pagans who have no hope of a resurrection. The apostle is not denying that they should grieve over the death of a loved one. Rather, he warns against excessive grief that signals a lack of hope in an afterlife, an expression of grief similar to that of the pagans.

The basis for hope is the death and resurrection of Jesus: "For…we believe that Jesus died and rose again" (1 Thess 4:14).

The baptized person can also expect to be raised up to life again. Paul appeals to this basic belief of Christianity that God, who raised Jesus from the dead, will also bring to life those who believe in him.

Paul contends that those who are living when the Lord comes again in glory will have no advantage over those Christians who have died previously (1 Thess 4:15). In his explanation of the coming, Paul uses apocalyptic imagery. Some scholars think that the self-manifestation of God at Sinai in Exodus 19 provides the imagery for Paul's expression of the Lord descending from heaven and the dead rising up to meet him in the air (see 1 Thess 4:16–17). God tells Moses: "Go to the people and have them sanctify themselves today and tomorrow. Make them wash their garments and be ready for the third day; for on the third day the LORD will come down on Mount Sinai before the eyes of all the people....Only when the ram's horn resounds may they go up to the mountain" (Exod 19:10–13; NAB). On the morning of the third day there were peals of thunder and lightning, and a heavy cloud over the mountain, and a very loud trumpet blast, so that all the people in the camp trembled. But Moses led the people out of the camp to meet God. Just as all the people go out to meet God, so Paul presents the coming of the Lord in similar imagery.

Another possible image upon which Paul may have drawn was that of an imperial entrance into conquered cities. The people of the city would go outside the city wall and line the roadways to greet the king. He would arrive with trumpet blasts and heralds of good news. He, with his courtiers, would enter the city first, followed by the people, who would join in celebration therein. Paul may have taken this horizontal imagery and shifted it to a vertical one to fit the coming of the Lord.[4]

Paul states that the Lord himself will come. The theophany described in the prophetical book of Micah provides a basis for this notion: "For see, the LORD comes forth from his place,/ he descends and treads upon the heights of the earth" (Mic 1:3; NAB). This passage stands in contrast to some Jewish apocalyptic writings in which the Messiah is not involved at all. Paul does not use "Jesus," but rather "Lord" to emphasize the risen Lord's return. The cry of command, the archangel's call, and the trumpet blast are apocalyptic images also found in the Book of Revelation. These images emphasize that the initiative for the return of the Lord is taken by God. That is why Jesus said, "But of that day or that hour no one knows, not even the angels in heaven, nor the Son, but only the Father" (Mark 13:32). The cry of command, or God's voice, initiates the rising of the dead. As is typical of apocalyptic literature, God's command comes through an intermediary, an archangel, the highest degree of angels. The trumpet blast is also typically used in apocalyptic writing.

"The dead in Christ will rise first" (1 Thess 4:16b)—that is, those who during their earthly life were associated with Christ, that is, believed in him, will also be associated with him in the rising of the dead. "Then we who are alive…shall be caught up together with them in the clouds to meet the Lord in the air" (1 Thess 4:17a). The rising up of the faithful into the air to meet the Lord is taken literally by fundamentalists. To interpret it thus is to ignore the literary form that is used by Paul to describe an activity of God that human beings do not fully understand.

Paul continues, saying that "we shall all be with the Lord" (1 Thess 4:17b). Here Paul uses the Greek word *syn,* which means "with" in the sense of "eternal eschatological being with Christ." This being "with" refers to a relationship that has already begun on earth.[5] In 1 Thessalonians 4:18, Paul bids the Thessalonians to "comfort" (in Greek, *parakaleite*) one another with these words. In ancient, nonbiblical Greek, the verb *parakaleo* was used for comfort with a view to overcoming grief. Paul has adapted this sense to his notion of comforting those who grieve over the death of loved ones. The consolation is based on the assurance that Paul's exhortation is "by the word of the

Lord" (1 Thess 4:15) and not merely on the word of Paul himself. Thus Paul ends his reassurance that those who are faithful to their Lord will be united with him for all eternity.

For Reflection

1. How do you think St. Paul's teaching on the Lord's coming is commonly understood by people today?
2. Do you find consolation in this teaching? Why?
3. What is the most consoling aspect for you in Paul's explanation of the Lord's coming?

Prayer For a Happy Death
Author Unknown

FATHER,
    you made us in your own image
    and your Son accepted death for our salvation.
Help us to keep watch in prayer at all times.
May we be free from sin when we leave this world
    and rejoice in peace with you for ever.[6]

III. SURPRISING RETURN

Preparation: Read 1 Thessalonians 5:1–28 in which Paul explains the unexpectedness of the Lord's coming and that people need to live their lives in such a way that they are always prepared.

> For you yourselves know very well that the day of
> the Lord will come like a thief in the night. When
> they say, "There is peace and security," then sudden

destruction will come upon them, as labor pains come upon a pregnant woman, and there will be no escape! But you...are not in darkness, for that day to surprise you like a thief; for you are all children of light and children of the day; we are not of the night or of darkness. So then let us not fall asleep as others do, but let us keep awake and be sober; for those who sleep sleep at night, and those who are drunk get drunk at night. But since we belong to the day, let us be sober, and put on the breastplate of faith and love, and for a helmet the hope of salvation. For God has destined us not for wrath but for obtaining salvation through our Lord Jesus Christ, who died for us, so that whether we are awake or asleep we may live with him. Therefore encourage one another and build up each other, as indeed you are doing. (1 Thess 5:2–11; NRSV)

This passage is somewhat like the first one above, 1 Thessalonians 4:13–18, but it differs in perspective. In the first one, Paul deals with what becomes of those who have died. In this passage, he deals with the coming of the Lord in view of those who are still alive.

"The day of the Lord" is widely used by the prophets in the Old Testament to express the intervention of God in history when God's power and justice will triumph. For example, Amos warns the people of Israel who long for the coming of the Lord and who believe that when he comes, he will punish Israel's enemies while rewarding Israel.

> Woe to those who yearn for the day of the
>   LORD!
>   What will this day of the LORD mean for
>   you?
>   Darkness and not light! (Amos 5:18; NAB).

Another similar example appears in the prophecy of Joel:

Blow the trumpet in Zion,
  sound the alarm on my holy mountain!
Let all who dwell in the land tremble,
  for the day of the LORD is coming;
Yes, it is near, a day of darkness and of gloom,
  a day of clouds and somberness! (Joel 2:1–2; NAB)

In the New Testament, it is Jesus the "Lord," in place of Yahweh of the Old Testament, whose coming will reveal his glory in its fullness. His faithful people will be freed from blame, and the world will be judged in righteousness.

We can assume that the Thessalonians were concerned about the time of the Lord's coming. They wanted to know when precisely their Lord was to come again so that they might be well prepared. Paul in turn calls for a lifelong preparation so that the Christian is not caught by surprise when the Lord comes. Paul reminds them that "the day of the Lord will come like a thief in the night" (1 Thess 5:2).

Paul warns the Thessalonians against a false security. One recalls the false prophets in the Old Testament who built up misleading assurance in the minds of the people. Jeremiah lays bare the deception of these fraudulent prophets: "'Peace, peace!' they say,/ though there is no peace" (Jer 8:11; NAB).

The pagans' adage was, "Eat, drink, and be merry, for tomorrow you may die." This attitude, however, is not appropriate for the Christian whose vision of the coming of the Lord is rooted in hope. Hope is grounded in the fact that Christ died and rose from the dead.

The suddenness and undisclosed time of the coming of the day of the Lord is emphasized by Paul's use of a second metaphor in 1 Thessalonians 5:3—that of the unknown moment of travail that comes upon an expectant mother. The Greek word for "travail" or "birth pangs" *(odin)* conveys a sense of anxiety and distress associated with an event.[7] In speaking of the day of the Lord, Isaiah laments the coming peril of the pagan nations who thumb their noses at Israel's God:

> Pangs and sorrows take hold of them,
> like a woman in labor they writhe;
> They look aghast at each other,
> their faces aflame.
> Lo, the day of the LORD comes,
> cruel, with wrath and burning anger;
> To lay waste the land
> and destroy the sinners within it! (Isa 13:8–9; NAB)

The complacent will not escape; ruin lies in wait for them who rather expected security and peace. Those who mask themselves in false security will be faced with certain judgment.

Paul makes a distinction between the willfully complacent sinner and his beloved Thessalonians. "But you are not in darkness…for that day to surprise you like a thief" (1 Thess 5:4). Certainly, a burglar does not warn victims beforehand. The metaphor of a thief sharpens the concept of surprise in relation to the time of the Lord's coming.

Darkness in early Christian literature was associated with sin and ignorance of God, whereas light was linked with divine revelation and righteous behavior. With their conversion, Paul asserts, the Thessalonians had become children of light. In 1 Thessalonians 5:5, Paul describes them as "children of the day." Therefore, they will not be caught by surprise at the day of the Lord. Rather than like a thief, that day will come as a friend to those who are faithful.

Nevertheless, Paul warns the Thessalonians to continue in their wakeful attitude. As Christians, they have been delivered from the darkness of the night. Nighttime and darkness are associated with drunkenness and other reprehensible behavior. At their baptism, the Thessalonians turned their backs on the pagan way of living. Metaphorically, they became sober (1 Thess 5:6–7). Every moment of their entire lives from that time on is to be lived under the expectation of the coming of the Lord.

So as to remain in their baptismal innocence, Paul exhorts the Thessalonians: "Let us be sober, and put on the breastplate of faith and love, and for a helmet the hope of salvation" (1 Thess 5:8). In the Old Testament book of Isaiah, the prophet spoke of the grief of Yahweh on seeing the sinfulness of Israel. God then took the initiative. "He put on justice as his breastplate,/salvation, as the helmet on his head./He clothed himself with garments of vengeance,/wrapped himself in a mantle of zeal" (Isa 59:17 NAB). Paul, then, borrowing the language of Isaiah, sets forth the virtues of faith, hope and love as the appropriate armor for the Christian.

"For God has not destined us for wrath" (1 Thess 5:9). Paul is not saying that Christians are predestined, but rather that they were destined for salvation by reason of their election to be among his chosen people. Hence, they are delivered from God's wrath because they are maintaining their relationship initiated by baptism.

Paul reminds the Thessalonians that they were endowed with God's glory; they live as citizens of heaven (Phil 3:20) rather than of this world. This grace comes to them "through our Lord Jesus Christ, who died for us so that whether we wake or sleep we might live with him" (1 Thess 5:10). The Greek word for "live" is *zao,* which conveys the sense of living eternally with the Lord.

Thus Paul encourages the Thessalonians to console one another with this Christian belief and to "build up one another" (1 Thess 5:11) as they are already doing.

For Reflection

1. Paul frequently speaks of thanking God. With what type of prayer are you most comfortable? Is the content of most of your prayer thanksgiving or petition?
2. When a friend or loved one dies, what action of the church is most consoling to you?
3. What does the coming of the Lord mean to you?

Prayer For a Happy Death
John Henry Newman: Cardinal, Thinker, Essayist (d. A.D. 1890)

O MY LORD AND SAVIOUR,
> support me in that hour
>> in the strong arms of the Sacraments,
>> and by the fresh fragrance of thy consolations.
> Let the absolving words be said over me,
>> and the holy oil sign and seal me,
>> and Thy own Body be my food,
>> and Thy Blood my sprinkling;
>> and let my sweet Mother, Mary,
>>> breathe on me
>> and my Angel whisper peace to me,
>> and my glorious Saints…smile upon me;
>> that in them all,
>> and through them all,
> I may receive the gift of perseverance,
>> and die, as I desire to live,
>>> in Thy faith,
>>> in Thy Church,
>>> in Thy service,
>>> and in Thy love. Amen.[8]

> **Summary of the Main Points in 1 Thessalonians**
>
> Paul clearly has a good relationship with the infant church, which he founded at Thessalonica. Grateful for their goodness, he nevertheless summons them to greater holiness of life. They are to express their love for Christ in their daily encounters with one another, always living concretely their divinely chosen status. Such a life is an appropriate preparation for the final coming of the Lord in glory which, Paul warns, cannot be calculated.

FOR FURTHER READING

Brown, Raymond E. "The First Letter to the Thessalonians," in *An Introduction to the New Testament.* New York: Doubleday, 1997, pp. 456–66.

Collins, Raymond F. *Studies on the First Letter to the Thessalonians.* Bibliotheca Ephemeridum Theologicarum Lovaniensium. LXVI. Leuven: Leuven University Press, 1984.

Marshall, I. H. *1 and 2 Thessalonians.* The New Century Bible Commentary. Grand Rapids, MI: Wm. B. Eerdmans, 1983.

Richard, Earl J. *First and Second Thessalonians.* Sacra Pagina Series 11. Daniel J. Harrington, S.J., ed. Collegeville, MN: The Liturgical Press, 1995.

First Letter
to the Corinthians

INTRODUCTION

*P*aul founded the Corinthian Church about A.D. 50–52 and spent about a year and a half there. Corinth, a port city, was known for its luxury and licentiousness. The city was the richest and the most populous one in Greece under Augustus, who made Corinth the Greek capital.

The community at Corinth was made up of diverse peoples of various social conditions— Jews as well as Gentiles, slaves and slave owners, wealthy and poor, educated and uneducated. They were divided by educational differences, by social status and by a variety of religious backgrounds. In Corinth, there was a Jewish synagogue as well as temples to various gods: Zeus, Aphrodite, Asclepius, Serapis, Cybele and others. Given these differences, it is not hard to imagine that a wide range of ideas was floating around in this infant church, ideas such as spiritual marriage, the claim that some enjoyed a superior understanding of spiritual matters and so on.[9]

The temple of Aphrodite, the goddess of fertility, love, and life, dominated the city. Aphrodite and her temple prostitutes, together with the luxury the temple provided, gained Corinth the reputation of being the center of immorality and vice. The term *korinthianize* ("to fornicate") was coined in that part of the world as an insult to anyone whose life was judged to be immoral.[10] Such was the city and inhabitants to whom Paul ministered and came to hold with great affection.

Probably many of Paul's converts in Corinth had frequented the Jewish synagogue, as that was a common practice of some Gentiles who lived among diaspora Jews (i.e., Jews outside Palestine). It may well be that Paul's first encounter with some of the Corinthians was in the Jewish synagogue. The Acts of the Apostles tells of Paul's speech in the Jewish synagogue of Corinth.

When he moved on to Ephesus, Paul addressed several letters[11] to the Corinthians that dealt with issues of concern within the community. As can be expected, it seems that some leaders within the community wrote to Paul asking advice on how to handle some of the divisive issues. Paul naturally wanted to end the strife among these people who apparently had only begun to understand the basic principles of Christianity. The essence of being a Christian was love of others as Jesus loved, love without exception, love that in its practice would bring about unity among the believers. To do this, Paul seeks to communicate his vision of unity and holiness to the infant church so that one day the Corinthians might experience the resurrection of the body.

Outline of 1 Corinthians

Greetings (1 Cor 1:1–9)
  I. Divisions in the Church (1 Cor 1:10–6:20)
 II. Appropriate Discipline (1 Cor 7:1–11:1)
III. Matters of Liturgical Assembly (1 Cor 11:2–14:40)
 IV. Resurrection of Christ and Christians
       (1 Cor 15:1–58)
Ending (1 Cor 16:1–24)

I. CALLED TO BE SAINTS

Preparation: Read 1 Corinthians 1:1 through 1:9 (see below). Paul immediately announces his major message: holiness of life for one who lives in Christ.

> To the church of God which is at Corinth, to those sanctified in Christ Jesus, called to be saints together with all those who in every place call on the name of our Lord Jesus Christ, both their Lord and ours. (1 Cor 1:2)

The basic message of the First Letter to the Corinthians is found in this opening address; the emphasis on holiness or sanctity stands out. The Corinthians are to understand that by virtue of their baptism, they were sanctified, that is, set aside for that alone which is holy, or separated from that which is evil. The sense here is that of holiness found in the Old Testament, which indicated that the sanctified person or thing belonged to God. Israel was a nation that God had chosen and set apart to be a holy nation (e.g., Exod 19:5–6; Lev 11:44–45). In the Old Testament, the "people of God" assembled to worship or to hear God's word were referred to as the *kahal* (translated into Greek as *ekklesia,* and into English as *church*). Paul's designation of the Corinthians as "the church of God" not only emphasizes their oneness with other Christians, but also limits their actions to those that are worthy of this designation. The individual lives of the Corinthians are to reflect this reality of holiness and their being "set aside" for that which is holy.

As a people set apart for God by Jesus Christ, who saved them from their sins, the call to baptism is a call to be a saint, to be holy. Because of this common call, there is a unity among them and all who "call on the name of Our Lord Jesus Christ," a phrase that recalls the Old Testament practice of calling on the divine name (e.g., Ps 99:6).

The call to holiness is unthinkable to many people today. To be good, yes, but to be holy seems a little farfetched for the average person. There is the fear that it could make one seem self-righteous to friends and co-workers. Could St. Paul then be asking holiness of a person who lives and works in the midst of many unbelievers in a world that is almost totally secularized today? In spite of the cost, this is indeed what the apostle in his letter, inspired by the Holy Spirit, is demanding of his readers. Nothing less than holiness is acceptable. Nevertheless, living a life of holiness requires courage beyond living the kind of life for which many people are said to be courageous. One who rescues a child from a burning building, for example, is proclaimed heroic. That kind of courage is acceptable and, in fact, celebrated in our modern society. To be called by God to be holy, however, to live a life of holy thoughts and actions requires another type of courageous response. Can other people accept that? Will they question the person's sincerity and perhaps believe that there is some basic evil beneath the behavior of one who strives to be holy?

Those are valid fears because in our modern world, having much more than one needs, being wealthy and achieving fame are touted to be social virtues. Have we ever seen a paid television commercial that sets forth sainthood as something worth investing all one's energy and money? Nevertheless, in spite of the world's values, which differ so drastically from those of the gospel, and because it is the Spirit who commands this sanctity, the Christian will find that grace will not be lacking for those who sincerely desire and ask for it.

It is impossible to achieve this holiness on our own initiative and efforts. As Paul says later in the letter, it is "God [alone] who gives the growth" (1 Cor 3:7).

For Reflection

1. Reflect a few minutes on the idea that you are called to be a saint. What fears confront you?
2. When were you baptized, or "set apart" for God? Put that day on your calendar as a special day to celebrate in some way.
3. In daily life, what implications are there for you in being "set apart" for God?

Prayer on Finding God after a Long Search
St. Augustine: Bishop, Doctor of the Church (d. A.D. 430)

Too late have I loved you,
O Beauty ever ancient, ever new,
   too late have I loved you!
You were within me, but I was outside myself,
   and there I sought you!
In my weakness I ran after the beauty
   of the things you have made.
You were with me,
   and I was not with you.
The things you have made kept me from you—
   the things which would have no being
   unless they existed in you!
You have called,
You have cried out,
   and you have pierced my deafness.
You have radiated forth,
   you have shined out brightly,
   and you have dispelled my blindness.
You have sent forth your fragrance,
   and I have breathed it in,
     and I long for you.

I have tasted you,
 and I hunger and thirst for you.
You have touched me,
 and I ardently desire your peace. Amen.[12]

II. You Are God's Own

Preparation: Read 1 Corinthians 1:10 through 6:20. Paul encourages the Corinthians to live a life worthy of their exalted relationship with God.

> For you are God's field, God's building....Do you not know that you are God's temple and that God's Spirit dwells in you? If anyone destroys God's temple, God will destroy him. For God's temple is holy, and that temple you are....[Y]ou are Christ's; and Christ is God's. (1 Cor 3:9, 16–23)

A field, a building, a temple—all metaphors for the Christian's relationship to God. First, "God's field"—an interesting figure of speech for the Corinthians as well as for every Christian. A field is subject to the owner's use of it. The owner can be creative in decisions about a field. He or she could use it to plant various kinds of vegetables or fruits to feed people or even for a lake to be used for fishing and pleasure. Still, the field might be used for an edifice, one for use in praising God, for a school to enhance the education of human beings, or for business purposes. Thus God's field is totally dependent on God for whatever happens to it. Therefore, Paul is challenging the Corinthians to be at God's disposal.

Paul then uses another metaphor, that of a "building," to describe the status of the Corinthian Church in relation to God. Like the field, the building is also God's. God has constructed this building according to a divine plan and placed in it the gifts necessary for whatever God has designed for it. Every human being was created according to the creative plan of God and destined through baptism to share eternal life with God.

Finally, the apostle describes the Corinthians with another metaphor, that of a "temple": "Do you not know that you are God's temple and that God's Spirit dwells in you?" (1 Cor 3:16) His readers were well aware that the temple was the location in which God was most present to the people in the Old Testament. Thus the point Paul makes is that the Christian community as a whole, as well as each individual, is the locus of God's presence. Whatever the community or the baptized person does either reflects the goodness of God, or it deflects it if one's actions are sinful. If his readers understand themselves as God's temple, they will protect that temple from the snares of Satan and the world.

As a church and as individuals in the church, they will strive for the holiness spoken of above because a temple is consecrated or set apart as something holy. To defile it by sin is unthinkable to one who values himself or herself as God's dwelling place. A temple is also something very visible. Thus the apostle challenges the Corinthians to be visible reminders of God and to reflect in their actions their awareness of this great privilege. Because they are God's temple, Paul exhorts the Corinthian Church to "shun immorality…because the immoral man sins against his or her own body" (1 Cor 6:18).

St. Paul points out that all human actions have their recompense. If one destroys the temple of God, Paul says, his or her destruction is inevitable, even though it be at the end-time. As a community, destruction of the temple can occur from within when there is division or lack of charity among the members. Just as the temple was not to be destroyed, so also must the temple of Christianity be preserved for God's glory. Paul tells the Corinthians that the lives of Christians should be such that people would regard Christians "as servants of Christ and stewards of the mysteries of God"; as stewards we must "be found trustworthy" (1 Cor 4:1–2).

Paul admonishes the Corinthians for having accepted lightly a case of an incestuous union among them (1 Cor 5:1–8). Such a marriage was acceptable to Gentiles, but the Corinthians were set apart for holiness at baptism. So important is it to be holy for God that Paul warns the Corinthians not to associate with "immoral people…," a member who is an "idolater, reviler, drunkard, or robber" (1 Cor 5:9–11). As Fr. Raymond Brown has stated so well: "Today correctives about sex are often dismissed as Victorian, but that gives her Britannic majesty credit for something that goes back to the first century in Christianity. Responsible sexual behavior in and out of marriage is a major issue in life."[13]

Why is Paul concerned about sexual morality? Because, he explains, "…your body is the temple of the Holy Spirit within you, which you have from God. You are not your own; you were bought with a price. So glorify God in your body" (1 Cor 6:19–20). Sexual promiscuity, so prevalent in our modern society, is contrary to our very nature and to who and what we are in relation to God.

For Reflection

1. You too are God's "field." One who owns a field can do as he or she wishes with it. What are some things God is doing with you and through you in your daily life?
2. You are also God's temple. What does that mean for you in regard to your daily actions?
3. What are some things that you need to do or be to be an open field in which God is working and to be a temple in which God is worshiped?

Prayer of Self-Offering to the Trinity
St. Theresa of Lisieux: Doctor of the Church (d. 1897)

O MY GOD,
    in order that I may be a living act of perfect love,
    I offer myself as a whole burnt offering to your tender
      love.
Consume me continually,
    letting my soul overflow
    with the flood of infinite tenderness
    which is found in you,
    so that I may become a martyr of your love.
Let this martyrdom make me ready to appear before you
    and at last cause me to expire.
Let my soul cast itself without delay
    into the everlasting arms of your merciful love.
O MY BELOVED,
    with every beat of my heart
    I desire to renew this offering
    an infinite number of times,
    until that day when the shadows shall vanish
    and I shall be able to retell my love
    in an eternal face-to-face with you. Amen.[14]

III. ADVICE TO SPOUSES AND THE UNMARRIED

Preparation: Read 1 Corinthians 7:1 through 11:1 in which Paul responds to questions related to problems that have cropped up in the church community since his visit there.

> Now concerning the matters about which you wrote. It is well for a man not to touch a woman.[15] But because of the temptation to immorality, each man should have his own wife and each woman her own

husband. The husband should give to his wife her
conjugal rights, and likewise the wife to her husband....I wish that all were as I myself am. But each
has his [or her] own special gift from God....To the
unmarried and the widows I say that it is well for
them to remain single as I do. But if they cannot exercise self-control, they should marry....To the married
I give charge, not I but the Lord, that the wife should
not separate from her husband (but if she does, let her
remain single or else be reconciled to her husband)—
and that the husband should not divorce his wife. (1
Cor 7:1–14)

Paul's practice of quoting something that came to his attention in a correspondence from the Corinthian Church (as in 1
Cor 7:1) and then responding to the issue is similar to the tech-
nique of Cynic philosophers of his day. Lack of quotation marks
in written Greek makes verses one and three appear to be con-
tradictory. If the statement that a man should not touch a woman
came from Paul himself, it would be opposed to his statement in
1 Cor 7:3 supporting conjugal rights between husband and wife.
As Raymond Collins indicates, "touch" was "a euphemism for
sexual intercourse in Hellenistic literature."[16] Thus it is generally
accepted by biblical scholars that Paul is quoting something from
the Corinthian correspondence to him.

Many scholars believe that this statement and Paul's response
to it indicate that some people in the Corinthian Church were
abstaining from expression of sexual love in marriage, thinking
they were spiritually strong enough to do so. Paul admits of a
temporary abstention from sexual expression of love in marriage on the basis of asceticism, but such ascetic practice should
be by mutual agreement, observed for a specified time only, and
for the purpose of establishing a closer relationship with God.

Paul points out that husband and wife have mutual and equal sexual responsibilities to one another.

Regarding marriage, St. Paul emphasizes that his prohibition of divorce is not just his teaching but that of Jesus himself. The only exception he admits is in the case of an unbelieving spouse who would leave the marriage. In such case, the believing spouse is not bound by the matrimonial ties. In Catholic theology, this situation is known as "the Pauline privilege."

Within the context of this passage on marriage, Paul asserts that each person "has a particular gift from God, one of one kind and one of another" (1 Cor 7:7). From that statement as well as his insistence on no divorce and remarriage, we may deduce that God gives the married couple the gift or grace to live marriage within the teachings of Jesus.

Paul regards each state of life as a vocation from God: "Only, let everyone lead the life which the Lord has assigned to him [or her]....So,...in whatever state each was called, there let him [or her] remain with God" (1 Cor 7:17, 24). How does the Christian know to what life God has assigned him or her? Paul does not say, but discernment through prayer and consideration of God-given gifts seem to be the logical path for Christians.

Regarding the unmarried, Paul speaks from the perspective that the *parousia,* that is, the Lord's final coming, was close at hand: "[T]he appointed time has grown short" (1 Cor 7:29). Marriage would make no sense in view of the absorption required in wedding preparation and the wedding itself. Therefore, St. Paul advises the single person to remain single so as to be concerned with things that would "please the Lord" (1 Cor 7:32), rather than with earthly concerns.

For Reflection

1. What is your specific vocation in life? What are the gifts God has given you to live that life?

2. What things in contemporary society contribute to and support adultery? What things can you do to alter this trend and advocate a more Christian approach to relationships and marriage?
3. The celibate life of priests, religious women and men, as well as lay single men and women, is not highly valued in our society today. How can you cultivate a greater love and appreciation for the celibate life in service of God and the church?

Prayer to Be a True Servant of God
Jon Amos Komensk (d. 1670)

O GOD:
   Speak to your servant
      and permit me to hear you.
   Tell me what you desire
      and let me find it agreeable.
      Give me the burden you judge to be fitting
         and assist me to bear it.
      Use me for whatever purpose you choose
         and help me not be found wanting.
      Command me to act in accord with your will
         and grant me the grace to do so.
   Let me be nothing
      that you may be everything. Amen.[17]

IV. THE LORD'S SUPPER

Preparation: Read 1 Corinthians 11:2 through 14:31. In this section, Paul gives instruction on liturgical assemblies, beginning with the celebration of the "Lord's supper."

[W]hen you assemble as a Church, I hear that there are divisions among you;...When you meet together it is not the Lord's supper that you eat. For in eating, each one goes ahead with his own meal, and one is hungry and another is drunk....I received from the Lord what I also delivered to you, that the Lord Jesus on the night when he was betrayed took bread, and when he had given thanks, he broke it, and said, "This is my body which is for you. Do this in remembrance of me." In the same way also the cup, after supper, saying, "This cup is the new covenant in my blood. Do this, as often as you drink it, in remembrance of me." For as often as you eat this bread and drink the cup, you proclaim the Lord's death until he comes. Whoever therefore eats the bread or drinks the cup of the Lord in an unworthy manner will be guilty of profaning the body and blood of the Lord. (1 Cor 11:18, 20, 23–27)

In the passage that we considered above, Paul paved the way for his account of the Lord's institution of the Eucharist. Only a temple prepared by love and charity is worthy of hosting the risen Christ in the Eucharist. Anything that profanes the temple profanes Christ.

In the time of the apostle Paul, the eucharistic gatherings took place in someone's home, usually a house big enough to accommodate a number of people. A house that large naturally belonged to a wealthy person. Probably there were several house churches in the cities where there were a good number of Christians. People who participated in the eucharistic meal brought food and shared it in common, something similar to the potluck dinners that we have today. It was in that setting that the Eucharist was celebrated. Because some of the members were persons of financial means, some of them tended to share the food with those of their own social status, thus leaving the poorer people to share what they brought among those of their own standing.

Paul cautions against such divisions that exist among the Corinthians who continue to come together to share the Lord's body and blood. They offend against charity by not sharing the food in common and even leave some hungry. Hence, Paul warns them that they divide the body of Christ and thus are not living the holiness for which they had been set aside.

In 1 Corinthians 11:23–26, Paul gives us what scholars believe is the oldest account of Jesus' institution of the Eucharist the night before he died. Scholars see this passage as one that Paul has received from tradition. Perhaps these words of Jesus were previously used in the liturgy of the early Christians shortly after Jesus' death and resurrection. Paul notes that he had received the tradition "from the Lord" and faithfully passed it on to the Corinthians when he was among them. He recalls this divine tradition to draw their attention to the abuses that surround the celebration of the Eucharist.

The supper is to be remembered as a covenant meal, which links them with God. "Do this in memory of me" means that Jesus' death, the result of God's love for us, is brought into the present and is proclaimed in and through the sharing of the body and blood of Christ.

> In so doing, we offer to the Father what he has himself given us; the gifts of his creation, bread and wine which, by the power of the Holy Spirit and by the words of Christ, have become the body and blood of Christ. Christ is thus really and mysteriously made present. (*Catechism of the Catholic Church* # 1357)

In sharing the body and blood of the Lord Jesus, Christians participate in the body of Christ. The Eucharist brings about a union of Christians with Christ. Paul notes earlier in the letter: "The bread which we break, is it not a participation in the body of Christ?" (1 Cor 10:16) Because of this union, therefore, Christians are "guilty of profaning the body and blood of the Lord" (1 Cor 11:27) when they treat one another with disdain. In such instances, the power of Christ for wholeness in the Lord is rendered by and for the sinner "a power of destruction"[18] (1 Cor 12:4).

Paul then moves into a treatise on charisms, or gifts. He notes that there are "varieties of gifts, but the same Spirit" (1 Cor 12). Because we are all members of the "body of Christ and individually members of it" (1 Cor 12:27), each person is graced by God to contribute to the health of the body. Paul picks out the gift of love as the charism supreme above all others, the topic of the following section.

For Reflection

1. Are you aware of divisions in your church community? What specific things can you do to promote unity in your parish?
2. Today there are some Catholics who doubt the real presence of Jesus in the Eucharist. What do you think is the cause of this disbelief?
3. How is the Eucharist related to charity toward others?

A Traditional Prayer: Anima Christi
(Source Unknown)

Soul of Christ, sanctify me.
   Body of Christ, save me.
   Blood of Christ, inebriate.
Water from the side of Christ, wash me.
   Passion of Christ, strengthen me.
   O good Jesus, hear me.

Within your wounds, hide me.
> Separated from you, let me never be.
> From the malignant enemy, defend me.
At the hour of my death, call me.
> To come to you, bid me,
> That I may praise you in the company
> > of your Saints, for all eternity. Amen.[19]

V. Love, the Greatest of Virtues

Preparation: Read 1 Corinthians 13:1 through 14:40 in which St. Paul speaks eloquently of love and reminds the church that all gifts are to be used for the good of the community.

> I will show you a still more excellent way. If I speak in the tongues of men and of angels, but have not love, I am a noisy gong or a clanging cymbal. And if I have prophetic powers, and understand all mysteries and all knowledge and if I have all faith, so as to remove mountains, but have not love, I am nothing. If I give away all I have, and if I deliver my body to be burned, but have not love, I gain nothing. Love is patient and kind; love is not jealous or boastful; it is not arrogant or rude. Love does not insist on its own way; it is not irritable or resentful; it does not rejoice at wrong, but rejoices in the right. Love bears all things, believes all things, hopes all things, endures all things. Love never ends.... So faith, hope, love abide, these three; but the greatest of these is love. (1 Cor 12:31b; 13:1–8a, 13)

Thus begins Paul's great treatise on love, moving from patience to love. Love is the most essential quality of the Christian's life, and St. Paul makes the point that all else is useless if love is absent.

Our most perfect teacher of love is the God who made us, for St. Paul insists that we were "taught by God to love one another" (1 Thess 4:9). There were three words for "love" in pre-biblical Greek. There was *eros,* which had various nuances but basically indicated a love that sought the other for the sake of one's own ecstatic experiences. *Philia* was a type of love that demanded a response or some obligation. Then there was *agape,* a kind of love that was not for oneself, usually a higher being's love for a lower being.[20]

The love that Jesus requires of his followers in the gospels is one that, when directed toward God, implied a total trust and commitment. It was based on God's own love for humanity—a love that was totally unselfish, even to the point of giving us his own Son, a forgiving love, a love that was merciful and totally inclusive. This "love" is *agape* in Greek.

Concerning love as *agape,* Paul says that it is based on the self-gift of Christ. When we were still without redemption, steeped in sin as we were, Christ loved us. He made us holy, sanctified us and thus made us capable of loving others in the sense of *agape.* We are able to love even those in opposition to us, not for what we can get out of them, but because they too are loved by God. It was for them as much as for us that Christ gave his life.

This concept of love is that of which Paul speaks in 1 Corinthians 13. The Corinthians had been too impressed with the gift of tongues, a kind of mumbling in which the Spirit prayed through them. They had come to look upon this possession of the Spirit in terms of social prestige. Paul points out that the gift of tongues without the gift of love makes one as useless as an echoing brass instrument or a "clanging cymbal," which provides no harmony whatsoever.

The gift of prophecy, or that of understanding the deep mysteries of God, or even faith that is powerful enough to remove mountains—great though these gifts are, they count as nothing without the virtue of love. The same is true concerning generosity, even generosity to the point of giving one's life as sacrifice (1 Cor 13:2). Without love, such generosity is of no value. All gifts of the Spirit are meant to contribute to the building up of the body of Christ, to bring unity among the members (see 1 Cor 12).

Beginning in 1 Corinthians 13:4 through 7, Paul points out two qualities of love, namely, patience and kindness, qualities practiced by God in dealing with humanity and which the Corinthians had violated in relation to one another. Then in 1 Corinthians 13:8 through 13, the apostle designates a number of other qualities and actions that stand in contrast to love. He implies that the Corinthians are still immature, but Paul hopes they will move toward maturity. Thus he sets before them faith, hope and love; the first two will not be needed when we see the Lord face to face. Love, however, will endure into eternity.

This treatise on love is one of the most poetic and beautiful of all Paul's works. Clearly, love (in the sense of the Greek, *agape*) has its origins in God. Paul refers to a person who disagrees with other members within the Corinthian Church as "the brother for whom Christ died" (1 Cor 8:11). God has prepared us to love as Jesus did. Paul tells the church, "you were washed, you were sanctified, you were justified in the name of the Lord Jesus Christ and in the Spirit of our God" (1 Cor 6:11). Divisions, Paul indicates, are a sign of the absence of love, and that void affects their worship when they come together as church (1 Cor 11:16, 23; 14:31–36; 15:1–3).

For Reflection

1. How is moral conduct reflective of love of neighbor?
2. What motivates you the most to live a life of love both for God and other people?
3. What might you do in your neighborhood or place of work to promote an atmosphere of Christian love and respect of each person?

Prayer for Harmony
St. Dionysius of Alexandria: Bishop (d. A.D. 264)

GOD THE FATHER,
> Source of everything divine,
> > you are good surpassing everything good
> > and just surpassing everything just.
> In you is tranquility,
> > as well as peace and harmony.
> Heal our divisions
> > and restore us to the unity of love,
> > and the ties of divine affection
> > and make us one in the Spirit by your peace
> > which renders everything peaceful.
> We ask this through the grace, mercy and compassion
> > of your only Son, our Lord Jesus Christ. Amen.[21]

VI. THE RESURRECTION OF THE BODY

Preparation: Read 1 Corinthians 15:1 through 16:24 in which Paul deals with the resurrection of the body.

> For I delivered to you as of first importance what I also received that Christ died for our sins in accordance with the scriptures, that he was buried, that he was raised on the third day in accordance with the scriptures....Now if Christ is preached as raised from the dead, how can some of you say that there is no resurrection of the dead?....But in fact Christ has been raised from the dead, the first fruits of those who have fallen asleep....Christ the first fruits, then at his coming those who belong to Christ....The last enemy to be destroyed is death....But some will ask, "How are the

dead raised? With what kind of body do they come?"... What you sow does not come to life unless it dies. And what you sow is not the body which is to be,...But God gives it a body as he has chosen....So it is with the resurrection of the dead. What is sown is perishable, what is raised is imperishable. It is sown in dishonor, it is raised in glory. It is sown in weakness, it is raised in power. It is sown a physical body, it is raised a spiritual body. If there is a physical body, there is also a spiritual body....Flesh and blood cannot inherit the kingdom of God, nor does the perishable inherit the imperishable. (1 Cor 15:3–4, 12, 20–27; 35–39; 42–50)

St. Paul begins this section of his letter with a reminder to the Corinthians that belief in Christ's death, burial and resurrection are basic tenets of our faith as well as the basis for our own resurrection (1 Cor 15:1–19). In the verses that follow (1 Cor 15:20–28), Paul deals with the implication that Christ's resurrection has for Christians. Christ was raised by God to new life. Thus he was the "first fruits of those who had fallen asleep," that is, he was the first fruits of God's harvest. Those who are followers of Christ then are the second fruits. Then in 1 Corinthians 15:29–34, the apostle takes up an issue foreign to our thinking today. The Corinthians were engaging in some kind of ritual in which the living were "baptized on behalf of the dead."[22]

In 1 Corinthians 15:35–44 he deals with the question of how the dead are raised. Two issues are important to his treatise. First, what is our resurrected body to be like? Second, how do we know we will have such a body? To answer these questions, Paul uses the example of a seed that is planted in the ground and springs up with a different kind of "body." Certainly, even by close observance of a seed, we are unable to know what the seed's plant form will be like if we have had no experience of such a seed and its growth before.[23] So also with the resurrected body.

Regarding the second concern, Paul draws on what he knows of Philo's[24] explanation of the reason for two creation stories in Genesis. According to Philo, the first story depicted the first Adam, who was the heavenly Adam. The second story portrayed the Adam of history who was a copy of the heavenly Adam. Paul seems to accept Philo's distinction, but he changes the relationship between the two Adams. According to Paul's explication, the first Adam ("first man"—RSV) was a historical person who became a living soul. The second Adam ("second man"—RSV) became a "life-giving spirit"; that is, just as death came through the first Adam, so the resurrection came through the second Adam (1 Cor 15:21–23).[25]

As a result of the "first fruits," which implies more to come, all those who belong to Christ will be brought to life again at the *parousia*. Paul explains the human body as "perishable"—that which was sown like seed. The resurrected body is "imperishable." Though sown as a physical, weak, dishonorable body, it is raised as a glorious, powerful, spiritual body (1 Cor 15:42–44). As Fr. Cerfaux states so well:

> The body of Christ, glorified at his resurrection, contained the fullness of the Holy Spirit, the source from which all spiritualization was spread throughout the world. The Spirit would envelop the bodies of resurrected Christians, which would become "spiritual."…Living matter is not an obstacle for the Spirit; it belongs to God, like the Spirit; no blemish can prevent it from participating in the qualities that bring it closer to God—incorruption, glory, strength, and spirituality.[26]

By the "spiritual body," then, Paul is referring to the human body that is "adapted by the Spirit of God for a completely different mode of existence."[27] It is this mode of existence that each faithful Christian awaits at the coming of the Lord Jesus Christ.

For Reflection

1. Many Christians have a great fear of death. Why do you think this is the case? What does St. Paul tell us that would diminish those fears?
2. Have you ever been close to a person who has died? What was your experience then? Did it have any effect on your own view of death?
3. The church's teaching of the Communion of Saints has proven to be a great consolation to me since the deaths of my parents and two brothers. Discuss this teaching. (See the *Catechism of the Catholic Church,* 1994, # 946–948.) Do you perceive this belief of the church as a source of consolation? Why?

Prayer for a Holy Death
St. Eligius of France: King's Counselor, Bishop (d. 660)

O CHRIST,
    Let me confess your name with my last breath.
    In your great mercy receive me
        and do not disappoint me in my hope.
    Open the gates of life for me
        and let the prince of darkness
        have no power over me.
    Protect me by your kindness,
        shield me with your might,
        and lead me by your right hand
        to the place of refreshment,
        the tabernacle you have prepared for your servants
        and those who revere you. Amen.[28]

Summary of the Main Points in 1 Corinthians

In this first letter to the Corinthian Church, Paul addresses the divisions in the church and qualifies them as profanation of the body of Christ, wholly unworthy of those with such a noble vocation to be holy people. For the married Corinthians to grow in sanctity, Paul exhorts them to maintain the bond of marriage as the Lord had commanded. As for the unmarried, thinking that the end-time was near and marriage preparations would be time consuming, he counsels them to remain as they are. Regarding their eucharistic meals, their holiness of life should be obvious when they gather, and Paul points out the peril of receiving the Eucharist unworthily. Death for the Christian, Paul indicates, is new life, a transformation from a perishable body to a spiritual one that is imperishable.

FOR FURTHER READING

Collins, Raymond F. *First Corinthians.* Sacra Pagina Series 7. Daniel J. Harrington, S.J., ed. Collegeville, MN: Liturgical Press, 1999.

Marrow, Stanley B., S.J. *Paul His Letters and His Theology.* New York: Paulist Press, 1986.

Montague, George T. *The Living Thought of Saint Paul.* Milwaukee, WI: The Bruce Publishing Company, 1966.

"1 Corinthians," *The Catholic Study Bible.* Reading Guide. New York: Oxford University Press, 1990, pp. 485–95.

Second Letter
to the Corinthians

∞∞∞

INTRODUCTION

*T*he two letters to the Corinthians differ greatly. In the first letter, Paul deals with various doctrinal and ethical issues with which the Corinthians were struggling. In the second letter, Paul seeks to define the authentic qualities and teachings of one who ministers.

Most scripture scholars today agree that the Second Letter to the Corinthians is very likely a combination of several Pauline letters to the Corinthian Church, which were written by Paul on different occasions. The conclusion that the letter is actually a collection of letters derives from the loose connections between the sections of the letter as we now have it. I will follow Jerome Murphy-O'Connor's divisions of the letter: (a) Letter I: Chapters 1–9; (b) Letter II: Chapters 10–13; Conclusion: 13:11–13.[29]

The first part of Second Corinthians (Letter I) seems to have been written in the spring of A.D. 55, about one year later than the First Letter to the Corinthians. The occasion of the letter was probably in response to news Paul had received regarding the intrusion by some Judaizers[30] into the ranks of the Corinthian Church. Their purpose appears to have been to attack the apostolic authority of Paul. In this first part, Paul makes allusion to a visit he made to the church at Corinth on hearing about these disturbances: "For I made up my mind not to make you another painful visit" (2 Cor 2:1). The first nine chapters then are principally conciliatory.

The second part of the Second Letter to the Corinthians (Letter II) was most likely written in the summer of A.D. 55. In this part, Paul defends his ministry and his authority. He attacks the intruders as "false apostles, deceitful workmen, disguising themselves as apostles of Christ" (2 Cor 11:13). Paul calls the Corinthians to obedience to the gospel that he preached: "Examine yourselves, to see whether you are holding to your faith....Mend your ways, heed my appeal, agree with one another, live in peace" (2 Cor 13:5, 11). He makes it clear to the

---

Outline of 2 Corinthians

Letter A (Chapters 1–9)

   I. Greetings and Encouragement (2 Cor 1:1–11)
  II. Paul's Change of Plan (2 Cor 1:12–2:13)
 III. Paul Presents His Case for the Authenticity of His Ministry (2 Cor 2:14–6:10)
 IV. Relations with Corinth (2 Cor 6:11–7:16)
  V. Paul Begs for Assistance for the Poor in Jerusalem (2 Cor 8:1–9:15)

Letter B (Chapters 10–13)

   I. Appeal for Obedience; Paul's Boasting (2 Cor 10:1–12:13)
  II. Preparation for a Visit to Corinth (2 Cor 12:14–12:10)
Conclusion (2 Cor 13:11–13)

Corinthians that his ministry was given him for the purpose of building up the church, not to tear it down.

Part I. Letter A

I. WHY DIDN'T PAUL SHOW UP?

Preparation: Read 2 Corinthians 1:1 through 2:13. The apostle explains why he did not go to Corinth as the church there had expected. He speaks of suffering in light of Christ's own afflictions.

> Blessed be the God and Father of our Lord Jesus Christ, the Father of mercies and God of all comfort, who comforts us in all our affliction, so that we may be able to comfort those who are in any affliction, with the comfort with which we ourselves are comforted by God. For we share abundantly in Christ's sufferings, so through Christ we share abundantly in comfort too....We do not want you to be ignorant...of the affliction we experienced in Asia....We felt that we had received the sentence of death; but that was to make us rely not on ourselves but on God who raises the dead....I wanted to visit you on my way to Macedonia....It was to spare you that I refrained from coming to Corinth....I wrote to you out of much affliction and anguish of heart and with many tears, not to cause you pain but to let you know the abundant love that I have for you. If anyone has caused pain, he has caused it not to me, but in some measure,...to you all....So you should rather turn to forgive and comfort him....What I have forgiven... has been for your sake in the presence of Christ,

to keep Satan from gaining the advantage over us.
(2 Cor 1:3–2: 11)

Before Paul addresses the question of not making a planned
visit to the Corinthians, a visit that was eagerly awaited at least
by some in Corinth, Paul paves the way for understanding. He
brings to light their common bond of suffering and sets forth as
an example to his flock his acceptance of his tribulations as well
as his reliance on God for his endurance.

Paul's faith and trust in God, in spite of the sufferings he and
his companions have endured since the last visit to the Corinthians, are obvious. The nature of the afflictions to which he refers is
not clear, but whatever they were, they never made Paul bitter.
Instead, he viewed them as a share in the sufferings of Christ.
According to the apostle, Christ's sufferings are perpetuated in the
church that suffers trials and persecutions for his sake.[31]

How can we explain the suffering of good people, which
many people refer to as "the mystery of suffering"? The explanation lies in the realization that the reign of God is not in its
fullness as was substantiated by Jesus' sufferings. Satan is still at
work in the world, but Jesus' victory over him will not let evil
triumph. Even if the suffering results in death, resurrection will
bring life eternal. Jesus was innocent, perfectly holy, and yet he
suffered the worst of sufferings. He demonstrated how we are to
bear afflictions in the present incomplete state of God's kingdom, which he initiated by his life, death and resurrection. In his
own life, then, Paul imitated Christ in his suffering and did not
rebel and become embittered. In fact, Paul blesses God: "Blessed
be God" (2 Cor 1:3), he prays, and even in view of his present
affliction, he refers to God as "the Father of mercies and God of
all comfort" (2 Cor 1:3).

Paul goes on to acknowledge that the Corinthians, in imitation
of Christ, were also enduring sufferings from some outside hostility (2 Cor 1:5).[32] He speaks of his and his companions' sufferings

in Asia in terms of "afflictions" and admits that they had felt "utterly weighed down" by them, so much so that they had thought that death was imminent (2 Cor 1:8). Paul explains that this near hopelessness for their lives and God's delay of deliverance was to make them rely on God and not on themselves during their deliverance (2 Cor 1:9).

Paul, however, is definitely confident that God will be merciful and spare them. He pleads for the Corinthians' prayerful intercession on their behalf: "You must help us by prayer, so that many will give thanks on our behalf for the blessing granted us in answer to many prayers" (2 Cor 1:11). Paul uses the Greek word *deesis* (which originally meant "need" or "lack") for "prayer" instead of *euche,* the more common word used in the New Testament.[33] I suggest that Paul's choice of the word *deesis* stresses the humility and human need involved in prayer of intercession. The word expresses the fact that by praying, we acknowledge our powerlessness and our need for God's mercy, help and intervention.

Like a good "father" to the Corinthians, Paul is capable of thinking beyond himself in spite of his personal suffering. He is concerned for this church that God has placed under his ministerial care. He points out that God does not abandon his children in their times of suffering. By sharing with the Corinthians the comfort that he himself had received, Paul encourages them by recalling that their sufferings are matched by God's mercy and comfort. He also reminds them that the mercy and comfort that comes to them from God demand the response of mercy and comfort to others. We cannot hoard these divine gifts; the authentic Christian must grant them to anyone standing in the position of need for forgiveness and understanding.

In the following lines, Paul personally carries out this reminder by exercising mercy and comfort toward someone among the Corinthians who apparently had been the source of some of Paul's grief and suffering (2 Cor 2:3), perhaps at the time of a previous visit.[34] It seems that the church in Corinth had punished the offender, but now Paul advises them to discontinue their chastisement. Because the Corinthians had received mercy and comfort from God, they in turn are to extend mercy and comfort to the person at fault.

Thus Paul explains that he was not an unfaithful slacker in God's service of the Corinthians. Rather, his reasons for having to delay his visit were justified. One reason was his own painful situation; the other was that his visit might have caused more pain for the Corinthians. In clarifying this issue and related questions, Paul uses this opportunity to help the church in Corinth to accept suffering as an occasion for a deeper relationship with Christ and to be forgiving so that Satan does not gain the upper hand.

For Reflection

1. In what ways or on what occasions have you been conscious of God's mercy and comfort?
2. When someone judges that your actions were motivated by something other than truth or goodness, how do you handle that? How is St. Paul a model for us in this regard?
3. How do you handle the sufferings that come to you as a result of incorrect or rash judgment concerning you or your actions? What do you find helpful in this regard?

Prayer to Pray Always
From the Church's Liturgical Prayer

HEAVENLY FATHER,
    your son taught us to pray with confidence
      when he said:
    "Ask, and you will receive;

seek, and you will find;
    knock, and you will gain admission."
Teach us how we are to pray
    in order that we may fulfill the command of Jesus
    that we are to pray always and never lose heart.
Grant us the gift of prayer
    that is our line of communication with you
    and with your Son in the Holy Spirit. Amen.[35]

II. "FRAGRANCE OF CHRIST" OR "ODOR OF DEATH"?

Preparation: Read 2 Corinthians 2:14 through 4:15. In this section, Paul presents his ministry in terms of spreading God's word. His ministry, fraught with trials, is nonetheless a result of his apostolic commission.

> Thanks be to God, who in Christ always leads us in triumph, and through us spreads the fragrance of the knowledge of him everywhere. For we are the aroma of Christ to God among those who are being saved and among those who are perishing, to one a fragrance from death to death, to the other a fragrance from life to life. (2 Cor 2:14–16)

Paul tells the Corinthians that God in Christ has triumphed over sin for all people, and in Paul's case, his sinful life before his conversion. Before his new life in faith, Paul's life was taking its own direction from his mistaken interpretation of the law. As a result, he waged persecution against anyone who believed that Jesus was both the Messiah, whom Israel had awaited for centuries, and the Son of God, who became one of us by taking on our human nature.

Christ's grace changed all that however. By his death and resurrection, he metaphorically leads Paul and all those who walk the path of the cross with Christ in a procession of triumph (2 Cor 2:14). The Corinthians were familiar with the triumphal processions of the Romans into the imperial city. A general who had led an army in triumph over an enemy would go in procession, be at the head accompanied by trumpet blasts. Following were those who bore the booty and those who were conquered, thereafter to be slaves or to suffer execution. Thus it is that Paul presents himself, a persecutor of Christians, as one conquered by Christ and now driven by his love as a missionary for Christ. God uses Paul in all his incompetence to spread his word just as God uses each of us, regardless of how unworthy we feel, to do his work in the world.

Paul speaks of his missionary work of evangelization in terms of spreading a "fragrance of the knowledge of him" (2 Cor 2:14). The comparison is similar to wisdom in the Old Testament whose presence is described in the Book of Sirach: "Like cinnamon, or fragrant balm, or precious myrrh, / I give forth perfume; / Like galbanum and onycha and sweet spices, / like the odor of incense in the holy place" (Sir 24:15 NAB). So precious is the message of God's love that Paul likens his mission to that pleasant odor of incense that rises unto the Lord!

The apostle's whole life is filled with Christ and his word so that his life is like a scent that pervades its surroundings. Christ is the source of that fragrance: "For we are the aroma of Christ to God" (2 Cor 2:15). Because of Christ in him, and because some reject him while others accept him, Paul is a "fragrance from death to death" for some people, while for others, he is a "fragrance from life to life" (2 Cor 2:16).

What is it that gives Paul the confidence that, in spite of his past life, he is chosen by God to be the "fragrance" of Christ to others? Paul knows that his own weakness is nothing in comparison with the power of the risen Christ. He is fully cognizant that his accomplishments are not his own doing. It is God who gives the "sufficiency": "Such is the confidence that we have through Christ toward God. Not that we are competent of ourselves to claim anything as coming from us; our competence is from God, who made us competent to be ministers of a new covenant" (2 Cor 3:4–6).

So it is with every person who engages in evangelization in response to baptism. He or she is conquered by Christ for his work. No one can claim to be too insignificant to be a co-worker with Christ, for it is Christ who chooses a person. It is Christ who gives each individual the sufficiency to be the instrument or his "fragrance" that pervades the ambient in which he or she lives and works. Whatever be the channel of our evangelizing efforts (whether it be our daily example as authentic followers of Christ, or spreading his word through catechesis in our own country or in another, etc.), for some people our evangelization will be an aroma pleasing to those around us. For others, however, the message may be received with hostility or indifference and thus be lost upon hardened hearts or deaf ears.

For Reflection

1. What do you understand by "evangelization"?
2. Because all baptized Christians are called by Christ to evangelize, what gifts do you think God has given you to be an evangelizer? In what ways can you spread the good news of God's great love for us in both word and action to the whole world?
3. Think of the most pleasant fragrance you have ever smelled. Is it possible that you, an ordinary person, could be like St. Paul in becoming a fragrance of Christ in the midst of others? Why do you think that God chose you in baptism to be his follower?

Prayer for the Gift to Seek God
St. Benedict of Nursia: Founder of Monasticism (d. A.D. 543)

FATHER, in your goodness
    grant me the intellect to comprehend you,
        the perception to discern you,
            and the reason to appreciate you.
In your kindness endow me with the diligence to look for
    you,
    the wisdom to discover you,
        and the spirit to apprehend you.
In your graciousness
    bestow on me a heart to contemplate you,
        ears to hear you,
            eyes to see you,
    and a tongue to speak of you.
In your mercy
    confer on me a conversation pleasing to you,
        the patience to wait for you,
           and the perseverance to long for you.
Grant me a perfect end—your holy presence. Amen.[36]

III. LIFE WITH A VISION

Preparation: Read 2 Corinthians 4:16 through 18. St. Paul speaks of the body "wasting away" in view of eternal life.

So we do not lose heart. Though our outer nature is wasting away our inner nature is being renewed every day. For this slight momentary affliction is preparing for us an eternal weight of glory beyond all comparison, because we look not to the things that are seen but to the things that are unseen; for the things that are seen are transient, but the things that are unseen are eternal. (2 Corinthians 4:16–18)

According to Paul, as long as one's vision is focused on the renewal that is taking place within by the power of the Holy Spirit, there was nothing to lose heart about in the wasting away of the body. This body that wastes away is likened to a clay jar in 2 Corinthians 4:7, an image that expresses the fragility of the mortal body.

That does not mean, however, that the outer nature has no significant role in this earthly life. To the contrary, it is the outer body that enables us to experience suffering, the "not yet" or the incompleteness of the reign of God. This outer nature enables us to "suffer with Christ in order that we may also be glorified with him" (Rom 8:17). The afflictions that we suffer are light, Paul claims, compared to the extraordinary degree of glory that awaits the Christian at the coming of the Lord. Previous to this passage, Paul speaks of his afflictions by which none of them is he crushed because in his body he carries "the death of Jesus" (2 Cor 4:8–10).

On the other hand, we are not to think of the outer nature as a shell in which the spirit is trapped. Our bodies enable us to relate to God and to other people; there must be an interconnection of the outer nature with the inner one. Nevertheless, the temporary character of the body, the manifestation of the outer nature, is a constant reminder that we are not citizens of this world, but that "our citizenship is in heaven" (Phil 3:20).

The outer nature prepares us for "an eternal weight of glory beyond all comparison" (2 Cor 4:18). The weight of the outer nature, in light of the eternal weight of glory, does not cause the baptized person to despair. Through the outer nature, we are made ready to participate in the fullness of God's glory, and through it we approach the holiness of God in the body of Christ: "For by one Spirit we were all baptized into one body—

Jews or Greeks, slaves or free—and all were made to drink of one Spirit....Now you are the body of Christ and individually members of it" (1 Cor 12:13, 27).

Through this outer body, we are also being transformed (in Greek, *metamorphoumetha*) into his (Christ's) likeness "from one degree of glory to another" (2 Cor 3:18). Usually one thinks of glory as associated with the world to come. For the Christian, however, the end-time events are already in action because Jesus initiated the reign of God on earth. In this sense the baptized person already shares in the glory of God through baptism.

Nonetheless, what the Christian awaits is not seen; that is, the fullness of glory, which we do not yet see, is forthcoming. The glory we now have in this outer nature is the Spirit's work within. Where there is a "down payment," there is assurance of something more to come. One knows by faith that there are things unseen that are yet received. One can easily distinguish between those things that are seen and those that are not, for as Paul points out, "the things that are seen are transient, but the things that are unseen are eternal" (2 Cor 5:15).

For Reflection

1. Why do you think people fear the "outer nature" wasting away?
2. What distinguishes the believer from the unbeliever in this regard?
3. How does the practice of euthanasia betray the role of the "outer nature" of which Paul speaks in 2 Corinthians 4:16–18?

Prayer to Be Clothed with All the Virtues
St. John Eudes: Co-initiator of Devotion
to the Sacred Heart (d. A.D. 1670)

O MY GOD, I magnify you a thousand times for all
your mercies toward me. Extend your mercies to all
the poor and take care of their needs. You have provided me with clothing for my body. Grant me also
clothing for my soul—your very self, O Lord. Let me
be clothed with your spirit and your love, your charity, humility, and meekness, your patience and obedience, and all your other virtues. Amen.[37]

IV. THE TENT IS FOLDING

Preparation: Read 2 Corinthians 5:1 through 7:16. Paul faces
the possibility of death with hope, and encourages the
Corinthians to reconciliation with him.

> For we know that if the earthly tent we live in is
> destroyed, we have a building from God, a house not
> made with hands, eternal in the heavens. Here indeed
> we groan, and long to put on our heavenly dwelling,
> so that by putting it on we may not be found naked.
> For while we are still in this tent, we sigh with anxi-
> ety; not that we would be unclothed, but that we
> would be further clothed, so that what is mortal may
> be swallowed up by life. He who has prepared us for
> this very thing is God, who has given us the Spirit as a
> guarantee. So we are always of good courage; we
> know that while we are at home in the body we are
> away from the Lord, for we walk by faith, not by
> sight. We are of good courage, and we would rather

be away from the body and at home with the Lord. So whether we are at home or away, we make it our aim to please him. For we must all appear before the judgment seat of Christ, so that each one may receive good or evil, according to what he has done in the body. (2 Corinthians 5:1–10)

Paul does not fear the fading away of the outer body. He faces death as a "going home." The tentlike body is that which Paul compared to an "earthen vessel" earlier in the letter (2 Cor 4:7). When he compares the present tentlike body to "a building from God," Paul emphasizes the durability of the eternal body or "building," a metaphor that conveys a sense of permanence. To further emphasize the immortality of the "building from God," Paul says that it was "not made with hands," and that it is "eternal in the heavens."[38]

Paul maintains that Christians are groaning; they "long to put on" this "heavenly dwelling" (2 Cor 5:2). "For as many of you as were baptized into Christ have put on Christ" (Gal 3:27). Paul is somewhat ambiguous in 2 Corinthians 5:2. Some scholars think that he is saying that an intermediate bodiless state after death is not appealing to him. "Here indeed we groan, and long to put on our heavenly dwelling" (2 Cor 2:2). Groaning is an indication of the believer's desire for the fullness of glory that is possible only at the *parousia* (that is, the coming of the Lord at the end-time). In Romans 8:22, the groaning of Christians is expressive of their eager expectation of the *parousia*.[39]

In 2 Corinthians 5:2, the groaning and longing are more specifically aimed at being clothed with a heavenly house or dwelling so that we may not be naked. In other words, Paul does not eagerly anticipate an interval between death and the *parousia,* when human beings would be clothed with their resurrection bodies. Actually, the Greek word Paul uses *(ependysasthai)* means to "put on over." Perhaps Paul is saying that he wishes to put on this heavenly body over the tentlike body, that is our outer body, so as never to be naked in between death and the *parousia* (2 Cor 5:3). Or it may be that Paul is saying that he hopes to be alive for the coming of the Lord at the end-time.

The apostle is certain that this earthly tent will be "swallowed up by life" (2 Cor 5:4). "The sting of death is sin" (1 Cor 15:55). Death will lose its sting at the coming of the Lord. God, Paul affirms, is preparing us for this clothing of life. We already have a guarantee of this promise in the Holy Spirit. The Spirit is the pledge that God's promise of a resurrection body will be fulfilled.

Nevertheless, as good as the thought of eternal life is, as long as we have the outer body, we are not at home with God (2 Cor 5:6). The Christian is not with God in this world in the same sense as he or she hopes for in the life to come. Although in possession of the outer body, the baptized person is in exile from the Lord, but she or he enjoys a faith-relationship with God: "We walk by faith, not by sight" (2 Cor 7:7). Once we have put on our "heavenly dwelling," we will behold God face to face. With that hope, Paul states that he would "rather be away from the body and at home with the Lord" (2 Cor 5:8).

Paul contends that, in the meantime, he makes it his aim to "please" the Lord "whether at home or away from home" (2 Cor 5:9). Logic would demand that a person would seek to please another with whom he or she aspired to be. The Christian, however, needs to be reminded at times of things that seem quite obvious. "The love of God," Paul contends, "controls us" (2 Cor 5:14). This love of God was revealed and proven in and through the death of Jesus on the cross.

The love of God was for Paul a determining factor in the way he lived his life, and so it should be with everyone who bears the name "Christian." It was that love of God that compelled Paul to give everything that he was in service of the gospel so that his Lord might be known and loved.

Paul's union with Christ in faith could not be destroyed by death. It would only bring him to a closer union with one whom he had served out of love although still in the "outer nature" (2 Cor 5:16). Paul's desire is that this be so for the Corinthians as well.

The very idea of being at home with God raises the question of judgment. "All of us must appear before the judgment seat of Christ" (2 Cor 5:10). Paul had reminded the Corinthians in his first letter: "Do not pronounce judgment before the time, before the Lord comes, who will bring to light the things now hidden in darkness and will disclose the purposes of the heart. Then each one will receive commendation from God" (1 Cor 4:5; NRSV). There is a reckoning for every human being for his or her conduct while on this earth.

For Reflection

1. What is it that most frightens us about death, even though it comes to everyone?
2. Reflect on your daily life. Were you to die tonight, what would you wish to change in the way you now live.
3. What do you most desire to do now in order to be more pleasing to God?

Prayer for a Happy Death
A Traditional Prayer

Jesus, Mary and Joseph, I give you my heart and my
  soul.
Jesus, Mary and Joseph, be with me in my last agony.
Jesus, Mary and Joseph, I breathe forth my soul
  in peace with you. Amen.

V. Where Is Your Treasure?

Preparation: Read 2 Corinthians 8:1 through 9:15. Paul praises the generosity of the Macedonians and encourages the Corinthians to be equally generous.

> We want you to know...about the grace of God which has been shown in the churches of Macedonia, for in a severe test of affliction, their abundance of joy and their extreme poverty have overflowed in a wealth of liberality on their part. For they gave according to their means...and beyond their means, of their own free will, begging us earnestly for the favor of taking part in the relief of the saints....Now as you excel in everything... see that you excel in this gracious work also. (2 Cor 8:1–7)

In 2 Corinthians 8 and 9, Paul spells out one specific way that the Corinthians can actualize their love and service of the gospel. In his first letter to the church in Corinth, Paul had already asked the Corinthians for assistance for the saints: "Now concerning the contribution for the saints: as I directed the churches in Galatia, so you also are to do. On the first day of every week, each of you is to put something aside and store it up" (1 Cor 16:1–2). Titus, one of Paul's companions in mission to the Gentiles, must have notified Paul that the organizational aspects for the collection they had previously set up with the Corinthians had since bogged down.[40] So it is clear that this is not the first time the Corinthians have been introduced to the need for financial assistance to "the saints."

Who were the "saints"? In the Letter to the Romans, Paul identifies "the poor" as being "among the saints at Jerusalem" (Rom 15:26). He notifies the Romans that he will stop in

Rome on his way to Spain: "At present...I am going to Jerusalem with aid for the saints. For Macedonia and Achaia have been pleased to make some contribution for the poor among the saints at Jerusalem" (Rom 15:25–26).

The situation that prompted Paul to beg for them is recounted in Acts of the Apostles. A prophet, Agabus, from Jerusalem went to Antioch and "stood up and foretold by the Spirit that there would be a great famine over all the world; and this took place in the days of Claudius. And the disciples determined, every one according to his ability, to send relief to the brethren who lived in Judea; and they did so, sending it to the elders by the hand of Barnabas and Saul" (Acts 11:28–30). Also in his Letter to the Galatians, Paul explains that in receiving his mission to the Gentiles, he and Barnabas were to "remember the poor" (Gal 2:10). By contributing to the collection for the "saints," that is, the Jerusalem Church, they would help bring about reconciliation between the Jewish Christians and Gentile Christians.

Why did Paul insist that the Corinthians contribute to the collection? The Corinthians were Gentile converts to Christianity (or to "the way," as first century followers of Christ called it [see Acts 9:2]). Moreover, because the Gentiles had received the gospel from the Jewish followers of Jesus Christ, the Corinthians' participation in the collection would be their response of gratitude (2 Cor 9:10–12).

This collection was also meant to build a bond of unity between the Jewish Christians in Jerusalem and the Gentile Christians. If the Jerusalem Church accepted it, it would be a sign that they approved the mission to the Gentiles and Paul's "Torah-free gospel." If they refused to receive the collection, it would signify that they rejected the legitimacy of Paul's gospel that did not require observance of the Law in order to participate in Christ's salvation.[41] Thus Paul felt that Corinthian participation was extremely important.

Paul uses the example of the church in Macedonia (which included three New Testament churches—Thessalonica, Beroea and Phillipi),[42] a church that itself was suffering poverty. In spite of their deprivation, they not only agreed to contribute, but Paul states that they insisted that they do so (2 Cor 8:1–5). The generosity of the Macedonians is described by Paul as an overflowing of "a wealth of liberality" (2 Cor 8:2). Of their own free will, they had requested to contribute since they had heard about the collections in other areas. He tells the Corinthians that he has been boasting about their readiness to participate in the collection, so if he should bring along one of the Macedonians and find that the Corinthians are not ready, he would be embarrassed.

The collection undoubtedly brings to mind the weekly collections at the Sunday Mass. Paul's second letter to the Corinthians is a challenge for Christians today to own the universality of the church. When there are extra collections for some aspect of poverty or disaster in another area or country, people sometimes voice their disapproval on the basis that the money is needed in their own parish or church. In the body of Christ, the church, each member is challenged to be concerned for people all over the world. As children of God, they are our spiritual sisters and brothers. Who among us would neglect members of our own family who might find themselves in a position of accepting donations?

For Reflection

1. What motivates you the most when you are asked for contributions to some situation of impoverishment?
2. Does your local church have collections for such situations? Is there a Peace, Justice and Human Life committee responsible for keeping the local church informed about cases of impoverishment both in your neighborhood and around the world?

3. What do you think of Paul's approach to convince the Corinthians that they should not only give to the collection, but give generously?

Reading on Serving the Poor
St. Vincent de Paul: Founder, Advocate for the Poor (d. 1660)

Even though the poor are often rough and unrefined, we must not judge them from external appearances nor from the mental gifts they seem to have received. On the contrary, if you consider the poor in the light of faith, then you will observe they are taking the place of the Son of God who chose to be poor.... We must take care of the poor, console them, help them, support their cause.

If a needy person requires medicine or other help during prayer time, do whatever has to be done with peace of mind....Do not become upset or feel guilty because you interrupted your prayer to serve the poor....One of God's works is merely interrupted so that another can be carried out.[43]

Prayer for the Feast of St. Vincent de Paul

God our Father,
you gave Vincent de Paul
the courage and holiness of an apostle
for the well-being of the poor....
Help us to be zealous in continuing his work.
Grant this through our Lord Jesus Christ, your son,
who lives and reigns with you and the Holy Spirit,
one God, for ever and ever. Amen.[44]

Part II. Letter B

I. In Christ's Strength

Preparation: Read 2 Corinthians 10:1 through 12:13. Paul appeals for obedience on the part of the Corinthians in view of his authority and an impending visit to Corinth.

> To keep me from being too elated by the abundance of revelations, a thorn was given me in the flesh, a messenger of Satan to harass me, to keep me from being too elated. Three times I besought the Lord about this, that it should leave me; but he said to me, "My grace is sufficient for you, for my power is made perfect in weakness." I will all the more gladly boast of my weaknesses, that the power of Christ may rest upon me. For the sake of Christ, then, I am content with weaknesses, insults, hardships, persecutions, and calamities; for when I am weak, then I am strong. (2 Cor 12:7–10)

In 2 Corinthians 12:1–6, Paul speaks of revelations that he has had. It seems that his opponents had boasted of their revelations, using them as an example to show their superiority to Paul. In spite of not wanting to boast about such gifts, Paul obviously thinks that it is necessary to admit to the church in Corinth his own revelatory experiences. Paul deals with the difficulty of possibly being misunderstood by the church.

Because of his many revelations, Paul alleges that he was "given a thorn in the flesh" (2 Cor 12:7). Scholars are at a loss to identify definitively the nature of the "thorn." Most likely, Paul has in mind his enemies because in the Old Testament, *thorn* is used in that sense: "But if you do not drive out the inhabitants of the land before you, those whom you allow to remain will become as barbs in your eyes and thorns in your sides, and they will harass you in the country where you live" (Num 33:55; NAB). In such case, then, Paul is saying that Satan has used his opponents in an attempt to disrupt the apostle's mission.[45]

"Three times," Paul comments, he had prayed to be released from the "thorn." This is the first time Paul has mentioned in all his letters that he prayed to Jesus for something, aside from 1 Corinthians 16:22 in which he prays "Our Lord, come." This is not to suggest that Paul was not a prayerful man, but it does emphasize the suffering that Paul endured from the "thorn." The mention of "three times" that he begged the Lord to release him of the suffering may connect the intensity of the suffering with the three times Jesus suffers and prays in the Garden of Gethsemane. Also relevant may be the practice of Jews of praying three times a day.

God did not, however, release Paul from the "thorn." God's answer to his prayer was that the grace given him was sufficient, and that "my power is made perfect in weakness" (2 Cor 12:9). The weakness that Paul was experiencing in dealing with the "thorn" makes obvious that it is God's power, not his own strength, that was at work in him and that sustained him through the ordeal. Therefore, because it is the power of God at work through his weaknesses, Paul states that he gladly boasts of them "so that the power of God may rest upon [him]" (2 Cor 12:9). Ironic as it seems, at the point of our greatest weakness, God does not abandon us but comes and dwells with us through the difficulties.

This phenomenon should come as no surprise to any of us if we stop and think about the way in which God's power works through our own weakness. It may be that we feel we are at our lowest ebb, when we become aware of accomplishing things for the kingdom that we had almost given up on before. On such occasions, we become strikingly aware of the power of God's grace.

Paul goes so far as to say that "For the sake of Christ, then, I am content with weaknesses, insults, hardships, persecutions, and calamities; for when I am weak, then I am strong" (2 Cor 12:10). As Paul Barnett articulates so well:

> Such strength is not automatic to weakness. Rather, weakness (as of the unremoved stake/thorn—v. 7) creates the human context of helplessness and utter vulnerability in which Paul the minister of Christ pleaded with the risen, powerful Lord—who himself was once utterly "weak," "sin-laden," and "poor" (13:4; 5:21; 8:9) in achieving our reconciliation with God—who is now strong in resurrected power to give his grace and power to the one who calls out to him.[46]

For Reflection

1. What is the "thorn" in your life that continues to harass you?
2. Do you think that your prayers during times of tribulation or distress may be answered in the way Paul's prayer was?
3. Are you able to help other people, who are experiencing hardships, to see their sufferings in light of the cross? To accept their own weaknesses in their inability to rid themselves of these sufferings?

Prayer for an End to Discord
St. Dionysius the Syrian (d. A.D. 848)

GOD THE FATHER, origin of divinity, good beyond all good, and fair beyond all fair, you are the abode of calmness, peace, and concord. Put an end to the discord that separates us from one another, and lead us back to a unity of love that may show some similarity to your divine nature. As you are above all things, unite us in one heart and one mind, so that through the embrace of love and the bonds of affection we may become spiritually one—both in ourselves and in each other—by means of your peace which renders all things peaceful. Amen.[47]

II. GET READY FOR A VISIT

Preparation: Read 2 Corinthians 12:14 through 13:1 in which Paul turns once again to his earlier painful visit. He warns them that they must correct their conduct for unity to occur.

[F]or the third time I am ready to come to you. And I will not be a burden, for I seek not what is yours but you....I will most gladly spend and be spent for your souls....Examine yourselves, to see whether you are holding to your faith....I write this while I am away from you, in order that when I come I may not have to be severe in my use of the authority which the Lord has given me for building up and not for tearing down. (2 Cor 12:14–15; 13:5, 10)

For a third time, the Corinthians are to prepare themselves for a visit from their spiritual father and founder. In the ancient Mediterranean world, children were expected to provide for their parents if they needed support. Even though Paul could have requested such help from his spiritual children, he refuses to do so; a refusal would have impressed the Corinthians.[48]

Like a parent, Paul will be happy to sacrifice himself for his fledgling flock that he holds so dear (2 Cor 12:15). He will willingly spend and be spent for them. Such sacrificial love will surely demolish any doubts concerning his love for them.

The letter implies that someone had called into question Paul's integrity. The person or persons had accused Paul of being "crafty" and that he "got the better of them by guile" (2 Cor 12:15). Dishonesty was not a part of Paul's makeup. Thus in 2 Corinthians 13:1, Paul declares that any charge they have against him must be substantiated by two or three witnesses. By this requirement, the apostle invokes the teaching of Deuteronomy 19:15 as a safeguard against false accusations: "One witness alone shall not take the stand against a man in regard to any crime or any offense of which he may be guilty; a judicial fact shall be established only on the testimony of two or three witnesses" (NAB).

Paul spares no words regarding these unpleasant matters. He states that he will not spare those involved (2 Corinthians 13:2). They seem to want proof of his apostleship, but the proof he offers them is ironic. He maintains that as an apostle called by Christ, Christ speaks through him. Christ, he says, is not weak; even though he was "crucified in weakness," Christ "lives by the power of God" (2 Cor 13:4). The Corinthians then need not judge Paul by his outward appearance of weakness, for his power is in Christ's weakness and hence is powerful. If he has to deal with such accusations when he arrives in Corinth, the apostle declares that he will deal with the persons involved through the power of the risen Christ.

Paul demands that the Corinthians look into their own hearts to ascertain the status of their faith (2 Cor 13:5). They must understand that Christ resides within them, as well as in Paul, and that their weakness can likewise be transformed in the power of their Lord.[49] Paul prays that they may be innocent before God.

Authority, Paul realizes, has been given to him by God for building up the Body of Christ. Any church leader, whether it be clergy or lay leaders, can take to heart this example of Paul.

The purpose of positions of authority is to hold together and make stronger the whole Body of Christ.

For Reflection

1. How can you aid church leaders in their mission to build up the Body of Christ? Consider leaders of parish or church committees, church hierarchy, and the pope.
2. Do you consider prayer for church leaders an important part of your role?
3. Sometimes church leaders at every level are criticized for maintaining the church's teaching on some matters. How can you respond faithfully in your role as a member of the Body of Christ?

Prayer for All Church Leaders

Lord Jesus Christ,
    watch over those who are leaders in your church.
    Keep them faithful to their vocation
        and to the proclamation of your message.
    Teach them to recognize
        and interpret the signs of the times.
    Strengthen them with the gifts of the Spirit
        and help them to serve their people,
        especially the poor and lowly.
    Give them a vivid sense of your presence in the
        world
        and a knowledge of how to show it to others.
                            Amen.[50]

Summary of the Main Points in 2 Corinthians

Because of internal evidence, the Second Letter to the Corinthians is considered by most scholars to be a combination of two or more letters of Paul. For convenience, we designated chapters 1 through 9 as Letter A and chapters 10 through 13 as Letter B. In Letter A, Paul explains why he had not visited the Corinthian Church as he had planned. He speaks of his sufferings in terms of his "outer nature wasting away" while his "inner nature" grows stronger in Christ. He also deals with the accusation that he lacked honesty. The apostle speaks of his evangelization efforts as spreading "the fragrance of Christ," a mission he received from Christ in spite of his weaknesses. His physical weaknesses, obvious in his "earthen vessel," are merely a sign that God is preparing a heavenly dwelling for him. He appeals to the Corinthians to take seriously the collection for the poor in Jerusalem.

In Letter B, Paul asserts and legitimizes his authority. He warns the Corinthians that when he visits, he will deal sharply with the perpetrators who are causing discontent with his apostleship.

FOR FURTHER READING

Barnett, Paul. *The Second Epistle to the Corinthians.* Grand Rapids, MI: William B. Eerdmans Publishing Company, 1997.

Best, Ernest. *Second Corinthians.* Interpretation Series. Atlanta, GA: John Knox, 1987.

Fee, Gordon D. *God's Empowering Presence: The Holy Spirit in the Letters Of Paul.* Peabody, MA: Hendrickson, 1994.

Lambrecht, Jan, S.J. *Second Corinthians.* Sacred Pagina Series 8. Collegeville, MN: The Liturgical Press, 1999.

Murphy-O'Connor, O.P., Jerome, "The Second Letter to the Corinthians," in *The New Jerome Biblical Commentary.* Raymond E. Brown et al., eds. Englewood, Cliffs, NJ: Prentice Hall Publishers, 1990, pp. 816–29.

Letter to Philemon

∞∞

INTRODUCTION

Of all the letters of Paul that we now have, the one to Philemon is the shortest—only 335 words. It is the only letter in the New Testament that seems to be a private or personal letter of the first century. When one reads the letter, the natural question is, "Why was this letter included in the canon?" It is speculated by some that Onesimus, the slave about whom the letter is written and who later became bishop of Ephesus, according to tradition, was influential in getting the letter included in the Pauline corpus. Others see it as an instrument of evangelization in the early church.

The addressees are: Philemon, a "co-worker" of Paul; Apphia, "our sister," who is probably Philemon's wife; and Archippus, a "fellow soldier;" and "the church in your house" (verses 1–2). Philemon was apparently a wealthy man because he had a house large enough to be used as a house church (see verse 2) and owned a slave named Onesimus. He lived in the lush Lycus valley, perhaps in Colossae.

The slave, Onesimus, had run away and eventually made his way to Paul in prison, where the apostle converted him. Because Paul and Philemon were friends, Onesimus probably knew Paul previously from association with Philemon.

Outline of the Letter to Philemon

Greeting (Verses 1–3)
  Part I.   Gratitude for Philemon's Faith (Verses 4–7)
  Part II.   A Plea for Onesimus's Freedom (Verses 8–20)
Conclusion (Verses 21–25)

I. Thanksgiving for a Friend

Preparation: Read Philemon 1 through 7 in which Paul thanks God for Philemon's faith expressed in love.

> I thank my God always when I remember you in my prayers, because I hear of your love and of the faith which you have toward the Lord Jesus and all the saints, and I pray that the sharing of your faith may promote the knowledge of all the good that is ours in Christ. For I have derived much joy and comfort from your love, my brother, because the hearts of the saints have been refreshed through you. (Phlm 4–7)

The greeting, verses 1–3, is addressed not only to Philemon, but also to Apphia and Archippus and the church in Philemon's house. The rest of the letter, however, is directed to Philemon personally. By addressing others in the church at the outset of the letter before turning to address Philemon further, it is possible that Paul wanted the church, if need be, to encourage Philemon in his responsibility as a Christian.

Paul provides a model for every Christian friendship. He maintains that each time he remembers Philemon in prayer, he thanks God for him (verse 4). One who thanks God for a friend acknowledges God as the gift-giver and hence gives glory to

God. One who prays gives the Spirit an active role in his or her prayer. Paul states in Romans 8:26 that "we do not know how to pray as we ought, but the Spirit intercedes for us," so when we pray for a friend, our prayer becomes the prayer of the Spirit as well.

In the next verses (4 through 7), Paul expresses in prayer his gratitude to Philemon for his "love and faith," which he has demonstrated "toward the Lord Jesus and all the saints" (verse 5). Thus Paul lays the groundwork for his request that Onesimus be freed by acknowledging that Paul considers Philemon to be a model Christian.

Paul also intercedes for him that Philemon's sharing of the faith will bring him to a deeper understanding of all the good that has come to them through Christ (verse 6). The love that Philemon has and the faith that brings to action his love are only a few of the gifts that have come to them in Christ. The apostle then goes on to express to Philemon the joy and comfort that he himself has gained from Philemon's love of others (verse 7). Philemon's faith, which has been demonstrated in love, has benefited not only Paul, but also the whole church.

For Reflection

1. Do you ever thank God for the spiritual gifts of a person whom you love?
2. Paul says that he has heard of Philemon's faith and love for the Lord Jesus and for other people. What are some of the ways you express your faith and love for Jesus Christ? For other people?

Prayer to Practice What Jesus Taught
St. Apolonius of Rome: Roman Senator, Martyr (d. A.D. 185)

O LORD JESUS CHRIST,
>   give us a measure of your Spirit.
>   Help us to obey your teaching,
>   soothe anger,
>   cultivate pity,
>   overcome desire,
>   increase love
>   cast off sorrow,
>   shun vainglory,
>   renounce revenge,
>   and not be afraid of death.
>   Let us ever entrust our spirit to the everlasting
>   God
>   who with you and the Holy Spirit
>   lives and rules forever and ever. Amen.[51]

II. A PLEA FOR ONESIMUS

Preparation: Read Philemon 8 through 25 in which Paul cleverly pleads for Onesimus's freedom.

Accordingly, though I am bold enough in Christ to command you to do what is required, yet for love's sake I prefer to appeal to you—I, Paul, an ambassador and now a prisoner also for Christ Jesus—I appeal to you for my child, Onesimus, whose father I have become in my imprisonment. (Formerly he was useless to you, but now he is indeed useful to you and to me.) I am sending him back to you, sending my very heart. I would have been glad to keep him with me, in order that he might serve me on your behalf during my imprisonment for the gospel; but I preferred to do nothing without your consent in order that your goodness might not be by compulsion but of your own free will. Perhaps this is why he was parted from you for a while, that you might have him back for ever, no longer as a slave but more than a slave, as beloved brother, especially to me but how much more to you, both in the flesh and in the Lord. So if you consider me your partner, receive him as you would receive me. (Phlm 8–17)

Rather than command Philemon to do what he wants in regard to Onesimus, Paul prefers to appeal to his love and goodness, which, from Paul's knowledge and experience of Philemon, have proven to prevail in the past. The Greek word for "ambassador" *(presbytes)* in verse 9 can also be translated "older man."[52] Perhaps Paul wants the word to convey both meanings, that is, that he as God's ambassador and as an older man makes this request of Philemon.

Paul tells Philemon first of all that Onesimus has become a Christian, one of Paul's converts in prison. He describes Onesimus as his "child," whom he has fathered into Christ. Paul has used the notion of spiritual fatherhood in other letters, too; for example, in 1 Corinthians, Paul maintains: "I became your father in Christ Jesus through the gospel" (1 Cor 4:15); and "My little children, with whom I am again in travail until Christ be formed in you" (Gal 4:19).

In verse 11, Paul makes a play on words using the name *Onesimus,* which in Greek means "useful." He tells Philemon that in the past, Onesimus was useless, but now he is useful to both of them. He has been transformed so that he is no longer what he was before—useless. Nevertheless, Paul will send him back to Philemon, even though Onesimus has become very dear to Paul: "I am sending him back to you, sending my very heart" (verse 12).

Paul writes that imprisoned as he is, he would have been glad to keep Onesimus to serve him in prison, but he would prefer that it be only with the free consent of Philemon (verses 13–14). In verse 15, Paul suggests that Philemon's temporary separation from Onesimus was part of God's own design in bringing Onesimus to believe in Jesus Christ. Paul's use of "he was parted" (verse 25), which is the passive voice, would in Hebrew designate a "divine passive." Paul, with his Jewish background, may very well intend this meaning, that God was the agent of the separation of Philemon from Onesimus.

Paul makes one last request of Philemon in verse 17; Paul's hope is that Philemon will receive Onesimus back as if he were receiving Paul, if indeed Philemon considers himself Paul's partner in the gospel. Certainly, if he were receiving Paul, it would not be as receiving a slave but as receiving a brother in Christ.

One is struck by the powerfully persuasive manner in which this letter is written. Paul seems to weigh each word so as to bring about the freedom of Onesimus. Freedom from slavery, however, is not the major issue that Paul is addressing. The issue at stake is the treatment of Christians for one another. In his Letter to the Galatians, Paul teaches the equality of Christians. We become one in Christ in baptism so that "through God you are no longer a slave but a son, and if a son then an heir" (Gal 4:7). "For as many of you as were baptized in Christ have put on Christ. There is neither Jew nor Greek, there is neither slave nor free, there is neither male nor female; for you are all one in Christ Jesus" (Gal 3:27–28).

This is the mindset from which Paul writes to Philemon. The new relationship that baptism brings about among Christians wipes out human differences and serves as a basis for Paul to ask for Onesimus's freedom. The challenge offered to Philemon is the challenge for every Christian to treat others as their brothers and sisters.

For Reflection

1. Perhaps Paul, by thoughtful reasoning, achieved in his letter to Philemon what he might have accomplished by other means as well. Would you agree with some writers that Paul was manipulative in his argument for Onesimus's freedom? Why?
2. Why did Paul not attack slavery as an evil institution in his letter to Philemon?
3. Have you ever had an experience in which you felt that God had intervened to bring someone to the faith?

Prayer of Praise and Petition
St. Serapion of Thmuis: Bishop, Defender of the Faith (d. A.D. 370)

> We praise you, invisible Father,
>> giver of immortality
>> and source of life and light.
> You love all human beings,
>> especially the poor.
> You seek reconciliation with all of them
>> and you draw them to yourself
>> by sending them your Son to visit them.
> Make us alive
>> by giving us the light to know you,
>> the only true God,
>> and Jesus whom you have sent.
> Grant us the Holy Spirit and enable us
>> to speak volumes about your ineffable mysteries.
>> Amen.[53]

> ## Summary of the Main Points
> ## in the Letter to Philemon
>
> In this short letter, Paul appeals for the freedom of an escaped slave whom he probably met while he was in prison. Because Philemon, the slave's owner, is a Christian and an acquaintance of Paul, the apostle asks that Philemon acknowledge Onesimus as an equal, given the fact that Paul has converted him to the faith.

FOR FURTHER READING

Fitzmyer, S.J., Joseph, "The Letter to Philemon," in *The New Jerome Biblical Commentary*. Raymond E. Brown et al., eds. Englewood Cliffs, NJ: Prentice Hall, 1990.

Havener, S.J., Ivan. *First Thessalonians, Philippians, Philemon, Second Thessalonians, Colossians, Ephesians*. Collegeville Bible Commentary. Collegeville, MN: The Liturgical Press, 1983.

O'Brien, Peter T. *Colossians, Philemon*. Word Biblical Commentary. Waco, TX: Word Books, 1982.

Patzia, Arthur G. *Ephesians, Colossians, Philemon*. New International Biblical Commentary. Peabody, MA: Hendrickson Publishers, 1990.

Letter to the Galatians

INTRODUCTION

Galatia, located in Asia Minor, had a history of annoyance to its neighbors. Invasion after invasion made the Galatians less than popular until Rome finally subdued them in 189 B.C. The Galatians remained faithful to Rome during the Mithridatic wars; thus Rome expanded the Galatian territory and made it a Roman province in 25 B.C. During the period of Paul's evangelization, a mixture of peoples, mostly of pagan backgrounds, populated Galatia, including Galatians, Greeks, Romans and Jews.[54]

There is not enough data to date precisely Paul's letter to the Galatian Church. It was probably penned about the year A.D. 54 on Paul's third missionary journey: "After spending some time there [Antioch] he departed and went from place to place through the region of Galatia and Phrygia, strengthening all the disciples" (Acts 18:23). The letter reflects the period in the early church during which some Jewish Christians were attempting to impose on Gentile converts to Christianity observance of the Law of Moses as a requirement for justification and final salvation. Scholars frequently refer to this group as "Judaizers."

While he was in Ephesus, Paul had learned that some trouble-makers, probably from Jerusalem, had gone among the new believers in Galatia and were trying to undermine Paul's teaching regarding justification by faith. From Paul's letter to the Galatians, it seems that the false teachers had insisted on the necessity of circumcision (Israel's sign of their status as the people of God) as a prerequisite for justification. It is to the new converts with their own unique background that Paul addressed his letter.

Outline of the Letter to the Galatians

Greeting (Gal 1:1–5)
  I. Perplexity at the Vacillating Galatians (Gal 1:6–10)
  II. Paul Defends His Gospel (Gal 1:11–2:21)
  III, Justification by Faith (Gal 3:1–5:12)
  IV. Exhortation to Authentic Freedom (Gal 5:13–6:10)
Conclusion (Gal 6:11–18)

I. What Stupidity!

Preparation: Read Galatians 1:1 through 1:10. Immediately after the greeting, Paul gets to the point of the letter. After he left, the Galatians listened to someone who preached a gospel contrary to that which Paul preached.

> I am astonished that you are so quickly deserting him who called you in the grace of Christ and turning to a different gospel—not that there is another gospel, but there are some who trouble you and want to pervert the gospel of Christ. (Gal 1:6–7)

An angry apostle pens these lines to the converts he had won in Galatia. Who are those whom Paul denounces for troubling the Galatians? The identity of the troublemakers is not totally clear, but from what we can gather, they are most likely Jewish

Christians from the central church in Jerusalem who still observed the Jewish law in addition to their faith in Jesus.

What were they teaching that differed so radically from the gospel that Paul preached? Paul's gospel message was that we are justified by faith rather than by good works. Chapters 3 and 4 appear to be arguments Paul makes against accepting the teaching that observance of the Torah or the Law is a requirement for full participation in the fruits of the mysteries of Christ's death and resurrection. Thus, their teaching was most likely a rebuttal of Paul's teaching that observance of the Jewish law, especially circumcision, was not a requirement for being justified. Justification was a loving and free gift of God, which could never be achieved by human effort. In his Letter to the Romans, Paul spells out more clearly his teaching on justification.

Nothing was more upsetting for Paul than for someone to distort the message of the gospel. In all the other letters of Paul, a thanksgiving follows the greeting. The absence of this aspect in the Letter to the Galatians is a signal to the readers that Paul is vexed with the Galatians. They have listened to another gospel—"not that there is another gospel," Paul comments (Gal 1:17). Instead of the usual thanksgiving, he begins by expressing his exasperation at them for having so quickly turned to another's teaching in his absence. The Galatians had received him with such tender care and now they forget so easily and turn to another person or persons who bring a different teaching, "another gospel":

> You know it was because of a bodily ailment that I preached the gospel to you at first; and though my condition was a trial to you, you did not scorn or despise me, but received me as an angel of God, as Christ Jesus. What has become of the satisfaction you felt? (Gal 4:13–15)

Even though the Galatians were new converts, Paul thinks they should know better than to listen to false teachers. He is somewhat harsh in his confrontation with the Galatian Christians: "O foolish Galatians! Who has bewitched you, before whose eyes Jesus Christ was publicly portrayed as crucified?" (Gal 3:1).

Perversion of the gospel was not unique to the first-century Christians alone. In fact, it is still a common phenomenon among Christians today. Because some people feel that the church is asking too much when it interprets the message of the gospel, they search for another interpretation that will accommodate their expectations. Some even turn to another religious tradition that they find less difficult to live.

For Reflection

1. After reading Galatians 1, how would you describe Paul's pastoral approach when he perceives that the gospel has been distorted?
2. What interpretations of the gospel have you heard or read that seem to be incorrect in view of church teaching?
3. If possible, look up Vatican II documents on the Internet and consult the church's teaching on some issue. (Simply type in "Vatican Council II Documents.")

Prayer to Remain Steadfast in Faith
St. Hilary of Poitiers: Bishop, Doctor of the Church (d. 367)

O LORD,
> deliver us from futile battles of words,
>> and assist us in professing the truth.
> Keep us steadfast in faith,
>> a genuine and unadulterated faith.
> Enable us to remain faithful

to what we promised when we were baptized
in the name of the Father,
   the Son,
   and the Holy Spirit.
Let us have you as our Father,
   and continue ever to live in your Son
   and in the fellowship of the Holy Spirit. Amen.[55]

II. BORN TO EVANGELIZE

Preparation: Read Galatians 1:10 through 2:21. Paul defends
the authenticity of the gospel he preaches. His gospel is not of
human origin.

For I would have you know that the gospel which
was preached by me..., I did not receive from anyone, nor was I taught it, but it came through a revelation of Jesus Christ....When he who had set me
apart before I was born, and had called me through
his grace, was pleased to reveal his Son to me, in
order that I might preach him among the Gentiles, I
did not confer with flesh and blood...but I went
away into Arabia and again I returned to Damas-
cus....Then after three years I went up to Jerusalem
to visit Cephas, and remained with him fifteen
days....Then after fourteen years I went up again to
Jerusalem with Barnabas, taking Titus along with
me....I laid before them the gospel...the gospel I
preach among the Gentiles....Because of false
brethren secretly brought in, who slipped in to spy
out our freedom which we have in Christ Jesus, that
they might bring us into bondage—to them we did
not yield submission even for a moment, that the

truth of the gospel might be preserved for you.... Those who were of repute added nothing to me, but on the contrary, when they saw that I had been entrusted with the gospel to the uncircumcised, just as Peter had been entrusted with the gospel to the circumcised...and when they perceived the grace that was given to me, James and Cephas and John...gave to me and Barnabas the right hand of fellowship, that we should go to the Gentiles and they to the circumcised. (Gal 1:10–18; 2:1–9)

Paul sets forth a defense of his qualifications for teaching the gospel that he had preached to the Galatians before the intruders had arrived. From what we can gather from the apostle's letter, some enemies of Paul had followed up his visit and had succeeded in convincing the infant church that circumcision and certain laws of purification had to be observed by the Gentile converts. These false teachers had persuaded the Galatians that Paul was preaching a watered-down gospel.

The apostle emphasizes that what he teaches is not a gospel taught him by human beings but, rather, one that was "revealed" to him. He speaks of his vocation to preach to the Gentiles in terms of being consecrated by God from the womb in preparation for his mission to the Gentiles. Two prophets in the Old Testament spoke of their calls in a similar fashion. Jeremiah (about 600 B.C.) was called by God in the womb of his mother to speak God's word to the nations:

> The word of the LORD came to me thus,
>> Before I formed you in the womb, I knew you,
>>> before you were born I dedicated you,
>>> a prophet to the nations I appointed you
>>>> (Jer 1:4–5; NAB).

Later, an unknown person, referred to as Second Isaiah, was chosen as God's spokesperson to Israel, sometime between the years 545 and 539 B.C. during the Babylonian exile. He preached that Israel was called to be God's servant among the nations and to make known God's glory and saving power to the whole world:

> Listen to me, O coastlands, pay attention, you
>   peoples from far away!
> The Lord called me before I was born,
> while I was in my mother's womb he named me.
> He made my mouth like a sharp sword,
>   in the shadow of his hand he hid me;
>   he made me a polished arrow,
>   in his quiver he hid me away.
> And he said to me, "You are my servant, Israel,
>   in whom I will be glorified." (Isa 49:1–3; NRSV)

Like Jeremiah and Isaiah, Paul also understood his call to be an apostle to the Gentiles as a vocation bestowed on him while he was still in his mother's womb. He was consecrated or set apart to be a great evangelizer to the nations of the Graeco-Roman world (Gal 1:15). The conviction that his call was a fulfillment of the prophecies of Jeremiah and Isaiah may have been the energizing force that enabled Paul to carry out his vocation with disproportionate zeal. Nothing seemed to deter him as he went from country to country, by land as well as by sea, suffering all kinds of hardships and illnesses, to take God's message of salvation to the Gentiles.

From a purely human perspective, one might conclude that in choosing Paul, God chose a person unlikely to succeed. Paul was a devout Jew "advanced in Judaism beyond many of [his] own age, so zealous was [he] for the traditions of [his] ancestors" (Gal 1:14). Wouldn't a better choice have been a Gentile who had already come to believe in Jesus Christ, one who was respected by both Jews and Gentiles alike? However, as is evidenced in both the Old and New Testaments, God's choice of people for important missions is most always surprising. Powerlessness, ignorance and lack of readiness are not obstacles to God's plan of salvation.

Paul tells the Galatians that after his conversion experience, he had spent three years in the Arabian desert. Only then did he go to Jerusalem to spend some fifteen days with Peter, and he had not even seen the other apostles. Obviously, that which Paul knew and preached could not have come from human sources.

To illustrate that Peter and the other apostles had accepted his law-free gospel, Paul uses the example of Titus, a Gentile convert, who accompanied him to Jerusalem. When he set forth his gospel to them, they did not require that Titus be circumcised. However, some Jewish Christians in Jerusalem who had learned that Paul did not include the Jewish law as a required observance for Gentile converts spied on them while they were there. Paul insists though that they made no inroads with the Jerusalem Church authorities in the condemnation of his teaching. They added nothing to his gospel, but they did request that he urge the Gentile Christians to help the poor Christians in Jerusalem with financial contributions. Moreover, Paul points out, Peter, James and John (the major figures in Jerusalem at that time) had extended a hand of friendship to him and Titus, and they affirmed that Paul's mission was to the Gentiles and that of Peter to the Jews.

For Reflection

1. By reason of our baptism, each one of us is called to spread the word of God. To whom do you think you are called to proclaim God's word?

2. How can you be God's spokesperson in the work place? In your home?

3. What are the difficulties you encounter in being a messenger of God's saving mercy?

Prayer for the Grace to Help Others
St. Francis of Assisi: Founder of Franciscan Order (d. A.D. 1226)

LORD,
> Make me an instrument of your peace.
> Where there is hatred, let me sow love.
> Where there is injury, let me sow pardon.
> Where there is friction, let me sow union.
> Where there is error, let me sow truth.
> Where there is doubt, let me sow faith.
> Where there is despair, let me sow hope.
> Where there is darkness, let me sow light.
> Where there is sadness, let me sow joy.

O DIVINE MASTER,
> Grant that I may not so much seek
> To be consoled as to console,
> To be understood as to understand,
> To be loved as to love.
> For it is in giving that we receive.
> It is in pardoning that we are pardoned.
> It is in dying that we are born to eternal life.[56]

III. "FOOLISH" AND "BEWITCHED"?

Preparation: Read Galatians 3:1–10 in which Paul once again berates the Galatians for having accepted another gospel that demands circumcision to be justified.

O foolish Galatians! Who has bewitched you, before whose eyes Jesus Christ was publicly portrayed as crucified? Let me ask you only this: Did you receive the spirit by works of the law, or by hearing with faith? Are you so foolish? Having begun with the Spirit, are you now ending with the flesh? Did you experience so many things in vain?—if it really is in vain. Does he who supplies the Spirit to you and works miracles among you do so by works of the law, or by hearing with faith? Thus Abraham "believed God, and it was reckoned to him as right-eousness." So you see that it is people of faith who are the sons of Abraham. And the scripture, foresee-ing that God would justify the Gentiles by faith, preached the gospel beforehand to Abraham, saying, "In you shall all the nations be blessed." So then, those who are people of faith are blessed with Abra-ham who had faith. For all who rely on works of the law are under a curse; for it is written, "Cursed be every one who does not abide by all things written in the book of the law, and do them." (Gal 3:1–10)

It sounds like the Galatians have "pushed a button." The fool-ishness of the Galatians is exasperating to Paul. He was the first to preach the gospel to them, and he had thought they were sta-ble in their faith, only to learn that they had been misled by "evil forces at work in their midst"[57] and had fallen under their spell. Paul was astonished, perhaps because he had left them with a vivid picture in their minds of Jesus Christ publicly crucified for their sins (Gal 3:1).[58]

Paul jolts their memory by asking if it was by power of the law that they had received the Spirit, or if it was by hearing with faith the gospel he preached to them. Of the five rhetori-cal questions[59] he asks, this one is the key to their problem. The

Galatians know that it was by faith in the message Paul had preached that they had received the Spirit, because good works in obedience to the law was unknown to them until the intruders had introduced it. As Gentiles, they did not even know the law when Paul first preached the gospel to them, so it was impossible that they had received the gospel through works of the law. Only now do they know it, perhaps by instruction of the troublemakers.[60] "Having begun with the Spirit," that is, by the power of the Spirit, "they began to live as Christians,"[61] but now it appears that the Galatians are willing to rely on "the flesh" (i.e., circumcision).

Paul stresses that it was God who gratuitously poured out the Spirit upon the Galatians, and the Spirit worked miraculous deeds among them. None of these miracles, however, were the result of the Galatians' good works. Rather, the miracles were gifts of the Spirit active among them. These gifts were pure gifts of God brought about in response to the Galatians' belief in God's word as preached to them by Paul, and not by anything they had done to deserve them (Gal 3:5).

Paul sets forth Abraham as an example of one who knew nothing about keeping the law before God chose him because God had not given the law until some 200 years later. Abraham, who accepted God's word with faith, was justified (or "made righteous") by God as a gift, because he put faith in what God promised him. In the case of both Abraham and the Galatians, faith, not good works, had been the determining factor in their justification.[62]

Paul maintains that scripture, which "foresaw" God's justification of the Gentiles on the basis of faith, preached the good news of salvation beforehand to Abraham (Gal 3:8). How can scripture preach? Paul understands scripture as God's word to us. Through the words of scripture, God's justification of the Galatians by faith is foretold in the call of Abraham in Genesis 12:2: "I will make of you a great nation,/and I will bless you" (Gen 12:2a; NAB).

This blessing reached the Gentile nations through the preaching and ministry of Paul. Those people to whom Paul preaches receive the blessing along with Abraham. Just as Abraham was justified by faith before the law came into existence, so too are the Gentiles justified by faith. If they begin to rely on works, they must observe all the works and practices demanded by the Torah. The Galatians would certainly be aware of the improbability of that achievement on their part. Paul has made his point well.

For Reflection

1. What similarities do you perceive between the Galatian Church and the church today?
2. What do you understand by righteousness?
3. What difference do you see between doing good works to express your love and gratitude to God, and doing good works to assure that you get to heaven?

Prayer of St. Augustine
Bishop and Doctor of the Church (d. 430 B.C.)

Breathe in me, O HOLY SPIRIT,
    that my thoughts may all be holy;
Act in me O Holy Spirit,
    that my work, too, may be holy;
Draw my heart O Holy Spirit,
    that I love but what is holy;
Strengthen me O Holy Spirit,
    to defend all that is holy;
Guard me, then, O Holy Spirit,
    that I always may be holy. Amen.[63]

IV. THE LAW IS NO SECURITY

Preparation: Read Galatians 3:11 through 6:18. Are the Galatians giving up their freedom in Christ for enslavement in the flesh through circumcision?

> Now I, Paul, say to you that if you receive circumcision, Christ will be of no advantage to you.... For you were called to freedom, brethren; only do not use your freedom as an opportunity for the flesh, but through love be servants of one another. For the whole law is fulfilled in one word, "You shall love your neighbor as yourself." But if you bite and devour one another take heed that you are not consumed by one another. But I say, walk by the Spirit and do not gratify the desires of the flesh. For the desires of the flesh are against the Spirit, and the desires of the Spirit are against the flesh; for these are opposed to each other, to prevent you from doing what you would. But if you are led by the Spirit you are not under the law. (Gal 5:13–18)

For the Galatians to trust that keeping the Jewish law of circumcision was necessary to assure their salvation was tantamount to declaring useless Christ's death and resurrection. Everything Paul had taught them before the agitators invaded their ranks would be worthless. They would be bound not only by the law of circumcision, but by the whole law, because circumcision was "a solemn commitment to a Jewish way of life which is characterized by nomistic service."[64]

When making reference to the law, Paul has in mind the Old Testament books that reveal the story of God's choice of Israel as God's own special people and the subsequent covenants made with her. These books of the law also defined the terms on which Israel's relationship to God was maintained. Along with the prophets, they were the guide for Israel's conduct so that she might remain faithful to God and be just in her relationship to other peoples.

Paul reminds the Galatians of their freedom. Theirs was not a freedom gained by observance of the law, but rather the freedom that Christ bought for them by his death and resurrection. They had been ransomed from their slavery to sin by the price of Jesus' life. Paul's own previous life as a persecutor of Christians was a reminder to the Galatians that he was not justified either through his own works, which in reality were contrary to the gospel, but rather he was justified through God's gracious mercy.

Paul taught that God had graced humanity with the gift of justification through faith in the risen Christ; it was not in response to their good works. Thus the apostle asserts: "So you see that it is men of faith who are the children of Abraham" (Gal 3:7). God chose Abraham to be the ancestor of his people. Through him, all nations would be blessed. One might question why God chose Abraham. Was it because of the good deeds he had done in observance of the law? No, God had not yet given the law to his people: "This is what I mean," explains Paul, "the law, which came four hundred and thirty years afterward, does not annul a covenant previously ratified by God, so as to make the promise void" (Gal 3:17). God chose Abraham because he accepted in faith God's promise of progeny, all the while knowing that humanly speaking it was impossible since his wife, Sarah, was barren (Rom 4). Abraham had done nothing to merit the blessing of justification.

The promise God made was made to Abraham and his offspring, but Paul makes the point that physical progeny counted for nothing. A real descendant of Abraham was one who accepted in faith that God's promises were fulfilled in Jesus Christ: "If you are Christ's, then you are Abraham's offspring, heirs according to promise" (Gal 3:29). The Galatians had made that leap of faith, and now they seemed to be backsliding. "For freedom Christ has set us free; stand fast therefore, and do not submit again to the yoke of slavery" (Gal 5:1).

Paul's adversaries, the Judaizers, added to the necessity of faith the need for circumcision and observance of some Jewish purification regulations and feasts. To Paul, this was totally unthinkable because Christ had achieved their salvation on the cross. Thus, he declares: "Even if we or an angel from heaven should proclaim to you a gospel contrary to what we proclaimed to you, let that one be accursed" (Gal 1:8). Later in the letter, the signs of Paul's anger blaze out at the Judaizers: "I wish those who unsettle you would castrate themselves" (Gal 5:12).

The freedom that the Galatians had received was not freedom to engage in an immoral life; that is, they were not free to engage in whatever occurred to them regardless of the morality or immorality of the action. Rather, their freedom was dependent on their fidelity to God and to service of one another.

Now that the Galatians have received the Spirit, they are to be guided by the Spirit. The Spirit will guide them in love for their neighbor, so that they do not advance their own interests to the detriment of others. Their love for one another is engendered by the Spirit, who will diminish the power of the flesh. Each person was bought by Christ, and hence no one has the right to "tear apart" one whom Christ loved so much as to give his very life.

Certainly, as Paul asserts, their love for one another would rule out the biting and devouring of one another (Gal 5:15), a lack of charity that the Judaizers may have caused. Paul's audience probably had witnessed beasts tearing apart other animals and perhaps people as well. Paul uses animal imagery to convey the destruction that occurs when human beings engage in uncharitable speech and behavior in the church community or even in families. Behavior that does not befit a Christian begins, metaphorically speaking, by biting one another; that in turn leads to divisions—the tearing apart of one another—and ends with their total spiritual destruction.

Paul was well aware of the tension that exists between life in the Spirit and life in the flesh. The life of the Spirit is always put to test in community, whether it be the church, some group that works for the church or even within the family. When we live for others, we discover the freedom that God has intended for both.

For Reflection

1. When we put emphasis on our actions as meritorious, for which we believe we deserve heavenly rewards in return, we make God our debtor. Does God really owe us anything?
2. What does "freedom in Christ" mean to you?
3. What do you find most helpful in living the life of the Spirit in daily life?

Prayer for Christ's Mercy
St. Jerome: Priest and Doctor of the Church (d. A.D. 420)

O LORD,
    show your mercy to me and gladden my heart,
    I am like the man on the way to Jericho
    who was overtaken by robbers, wounded and
        left half-dead.
O GOOD SAMARITAN,
    come to my aid.
    I am like the sheep that went astray.
O GOOD SHEPHERD,
    Seek me out and bring me home in accord with
        your will.
    Let me dwell in your house
    all the days of my life
    and praise you for ever and ever
    with those who are there. Amen.[65]

**Summary of the Main Points
in the Letter to the Galatians**

The Letter to the Galatians expresses for this young church Paul's disappointment in their acceptance of another interpretation of the gospel, one that was false. He sets forth in the example of Abraham's being justified (or brought into right relationship with God) that which had occurred in the case of the Galatians when by grace they received the message of salvation. He delineates for them the absurdity of trying to earn the gift of salvation by circumcision and observance of Jewish purification laws. Such action on their part is to proclaim useless Christ's gift of his life on the cross for their sins.

FOR FURTHER READING

Barclay, William. *The Letters to the Galatians and Ephesians.* Revised Edition. Philadelphia, PA: The Westminster Press, 1977.

Fitzmyer, Joseph A., "The Letter to the Galatians" in *The New Jerome Biblical Commentary.* Raymond E. Brown et al, eds. Englewood Cliffs, NJ: Prentice Hall, 1990, pp. 780–90.

Marrow, Stanley B. *Paul His Letters and His Theology: An Introduction to Paul's Epistles.* Mahwah, NJ: Paulist Press, 1986, pp. 83–111.

Matera, Frank J. *Galatians.* Sacra Pagina Series 9. Collegeville, MN: The Liturgical Press, 1992.

Letter to the Philippians

INTRODUCTION

The city of Philippi was located near one of the major Macedonian trade routes north of Thessalonica. The church at Philippi was the first Christian community that Paul founded in Europe. In Paul's time, the city was one of importance in Macedonia (which today is northern Greece). Philippi had been designated a Roman province under Octavian, who settled many retired Roman soldiers and their families there.[66]

As the Acts of the Apostles recounts, Paul, Timothy and Silas, along with other co-workers, visited Philippi on Paul's second missionary journey to the Gentile world, in about A.D. 50 (see Acts 16:11–40). According to this account, Paul won an influential business woman, Lydia, to faith in Christ and exorcised a slave girl. After an earthquake and subsequent imprisonment, during which time Paul and Silas baptized the jailer and his family, the apostle and his companion were forced to leave the city. They then went to Thessalonica, and those who had come to believe in Christ continued to support Paul financially.

Paul wrote to the Philippians from prison, possibly in Ephesus during his third missionary journey. Even though there is no personal confirmation of an imprisonment in that city, Paul does refer to multiple imprisonments in 2 Corinthians 11:23

and speaks metaphorically of fighting "wild beasts" in Ephesus (1 Cor 15:30–32). Because Ephesus was easily reached by sea from Philippi, his comment about visiting them again would be realizable.

Outline of the Letter to the Philippians

Greetings, Thanksgiving and Prayer (Phil 1:1–11)
  I. Personal News and Exhortations to Unity (Phil 1:12–2:18)
  II. Danger of False Teachers and the Need for Unity (Phil 3:1–4:9)
  III. Gratitude for the Philippians' Generosity (Phil 4:10–20)
Conclusions (Phil 4:21–23)

I. Joy Even in Difficulties

Preparation: Read Philippians 1:1 through 1:11. Paul opens this letter by expressing his deep love for the Philippians.

I thank my God in all my remembrance of you, always in every prayer of mine for you all making my prayer with joy, thankful for your partnership in the gospel from the first day until now. And I am sure that he who began a good work in you will bring it to completion at the day of Jesus Christ. It is right for me to feel thus about you all, because I hold you in my heart, for you are all partakers with me of grace, both in my imprisonment and in the defense and confirmation of the gospel. For God is my witness, how I yearn for you all with the affection of Christ

Jesus....Whether in pretence or in truth, Christ is
proclaimed; and in that I rejoice....(Phil 1:3–8, 18)

The gentle tone of Paul's letter illustrates Paul's tender feel-
ings toward the Philippians: prayer of thankfulness for the
Philippians; gratitude for their partnership in his ministry; holding them in his heart; and longing for them (Phil 1:2–5). Even
the thought of them brings Paul to grateful prayer. He refers to
the Philippians as "my joy and my crown" (Phil 4:1).

Considering that Paul is in prison, the letter is very upbeat.
It shows that he can take the worst of situations and turn it
into a positive force for taking the gospel to the Gentiles and
an opportunity to grow in his relationship to Christ. There is
no doubt that the focus of Paul's life was Christ and the
church.

Even in prison, Paul is concerned for the church rather than
for himself. He experiences joy in praying for the Philippians,
and he prays that love among the members of the church at
Philippi might grow more and more (Phil 1:3–9).

In his sufferings, Paul remains Christ centered. His whole life
revolves around Christ and his desire to make the gospel known
to all. The apostle is confident that the success of the gospel,
which he previously introduced to the Philippians, is not
dependent on him but rather on Christ. Paul began the "good
work," but it is God who will bring it to full completion on the
"day of Jesus Christ," that is, at his final coming. If he must be
away from them, he knows that God can use even that absence
to further the gospel. Paul trusts that his imprisonment is not in
vain nor are the intercessions of the Philippians on his behalf.
"For I know that through your prayers and the help of the Spirit
of Jesus Christ this will turn out for my deliverance" (Phil 1:19).
"Deliverance" for Paul could go one of two ways: He could be
delivered from prison, or he could be delivered from the flesh to
be with his Lord.

By praying for the Philippians, Paul sets an example for the church members in their relationships with one another. Ongoing prayer in response to a relationship is a demonstration of a mutual affection that is especially fitting between spouses, parents and children and between friends. Prayer for another strengthens family and friendship bonds because it shows a trust that God is the origin and goal of all ties that are good. "For Paul, *chara* is the joy of faith."[67] Paul is a witness to the joy (*chara* in Greek; see Phil 1:4) that characterizes the inner being of an authentic Christian, regardless of her or his misfortunes or situation in life. Joy embraces happiness as well as sorrow in the heart of St. Paul because his joy results from faith that God, who knows both the beginning and the end of events, reigns over all.[68] The apostle has faith that God will bring forth fruits of the resurrection from both the pleasant and the unpleasant. He can say, therefore, that his imprisonment "has really served to advance the gospel" (Phil 1:12).

In this short letter, the word *joy* or *rejoice* appears fourteen times. Three times, Paul urges the Philippians to "rejoice in the Lord." In announcing to them that he is sending Epaphroditus to them, he writes: "So receive him in the Lord with all joy; and honor such ones, for he nearly died for the work of Christ, risking his life to complete your service to me. Finally,…rejoice in the Lord" (Phil 2:29–3:1). Again he urges them: "Rejoice in the Lord always; again I will say, Rejoice" (Phil 4:4), and "I rejoice in the Lord" (Phil 4:10).

Paul faces life's difficulties and setbacks with faith. He does not allow them to dampen his spirits; rather, he looks upon them as opportunities: "I want you to know, brethren, that what has happened to me has really served to advance the gospel" (Phil 1:12). He notes that his situation has been an opportunity for the guards to know that he is there for the sake of Christ. It is also an occasion for others of his acquaintance to become bolder in professing Christ: "It has become known throughout the whole praetorian guard and to all the rest that my imprisonment is for Christ; and most of the brethren have been made confident in the Lord because of my imprisonment, and are much more bold to speak the word of God without fear" (Phil 1:13–14).

One of Paul's joys derives from the fact that the Philippians are partners with him in the gospel (Phil 1:5). There was no firmer basis for a deep and lasting relationship than sharing in the mission of making known the good news that God has acted through Jesus to save all people and thus restore their relationship with God.

For Reflection

1. Sometimes people are hesitant to express emotions of love for another, even for a spouse or for one's children. Do you experience such hesitancy, and, if so, why is that the case?
2. Everyone faces difficulties of one kind or another in daily life. Recall to mind one such adversity or circumstance, and think of some way to look at it as an opportunity to grow in your love for Christ.
3. Pope John Paul II reiterates the Second Vatican Council's teaching that all baptized persons have both the right and obligation "to strive so that the divine message of salvation may be known and accepted by all people throughout the world."[69] In what concrete ways can you exercise this right and obligation in your daily life?

Prayer for the Conversion of Unbelievers
St. Francis Xavier: Priest and Martyr (d. A.D. 1552)

O GOD
    of all peoples on the earth,
    be mindful of the many unbelievers.

They have been created in your image,
yet they do not know you
or your son Jesus Christ,
    their Savior who died for them.
By the prayers and labors of your Church,
may they be freed from all ignorance and unbelief
    and led to worship you.
We ask this through Jesus Christ, your Son our Lord,
    whom you sent to be the resurrection and the life
    of all human beings.[70]

II. Nothing Disturbs Paul

Preparation: Read Philippians 1:12 through 2:18 in which
Paul shares his contentment with whatever is God's will for him
and exhorts the Philippians to steadfastness, humility, selflessness
and obedience in imitation of Jesus, the Lord.

I know that through your prayers and the help of the
Spirit of Jesus this will turn out for my deliverance, so
it is my eager expectation and hope that I shall not be
at all ashamed, but that with full courage now as
always Christ will be honored in my body, whether
by life or by death. For to me to live is Christ, and to
die is gain. If it is to be life in the flesh, that means
fruitful labor for me. Yet which I shall choose I cannot
tell. I am hard pressed between the two. My desire is
to depart and be with Christ, for that is far better. But
to remain in the flesh is more necessary on your
account....If there is any encouragement in Christ,
any incentive of love, any participation in the Spirit,
any affection and sympathy, complete my joy by
being of the same mind, having the same love, being

in full accord and of one mind. Do nothing from self-ishness or conceit, but in humility count others better than yourselves. Let each of you look not only to his own interests, but also to the interests of others. Have this in mind among yourselves, which is yours in Christ Jesus, who, though he was in the form of God, did not count equality with God a thing to be grasped, but emptied himself, taking the form of a servant, being born in the likeness of men. And being found in human form he humbled himself and became obedient unto death, even death on a cross. Therefore God has highly exalted him and bestowed on him the name which is above every name, that at the name of Jesus every knee should bow, in heaven and on earth and under the earth, and every tongue confess that Jesus Christ is Lord, to the glory of God, the Father. (Phil 1:19–24; 2:1–11)

Paul knows that there are people in the Christian community who perhaps have ulterior motives for proclaiming the gospel, but the very fact that Christ is preached gives Paul great joy. As one scholar states: "For when the Word of God is preached it overcomes all hindrances and moves on to its goal; its contents are irresistible....The power of the gospel, therefore, does not depend on the character of the preacher."[71]

As he writes from prison, Paul acknowledges that execution lurks as a possibility for him just as his release is also a possibility. Both are very attractive to Paul. His great desire to be with Christ seems to be just as great as continuing to live in service of the Lord among the Philippians. The thought of both gives him great joy (Phil 1:18).

As Paul reflects on the two possibilities, he is convinced that if his life is spared, then his mission of spreading the gospel will continue unhindered. If, on the other hand, he is put to death, that also is consoling because eternal life means being with the Lord (Phil 1:23). Paul reasons that Christ would gain from his execution as well because martyrdom would preach its own message and Christ would be honored (Phil 1:19–20). Nevertheless, he is fully aware that his life lies within the providence of God and that nothing can really harm him unless God so allows.

The apostle maintains that "To live is Christ" (Phil 1:21); in other words, the whole of Paul's life is summed up in Christ. He looks upon his life and all its events, both negative and positive, as filled with Christ, and everything Paul does is done for him. All his joys and all his sufferings and difficulties play a role in his mission to take Christ to the Gentiles. Therefore, whatever his imprisonment brings in the end, God, and hence Paul as well, will be the winner. Whether it be life or death, both will be as life to Paul because neither can separate him from Christ.

Paul reminds the infant church that because its members have experienced the love, mercy and compassion of God in Christ, then certainly their love, mercy and compassion must embrace one another so that unity might be achieved. Unity can exist in a family, a community, a church and the world only if there is humility, self-sacrifice and a habit of putting the needs of others before one's own. Selfishness is divisive and turns one inward instead of focusing one's mind on Christ and his body, the church.

Paul's notion of humility has its basis in the Old Testament where it designates lowliness, insignificance, oppression or baseness. Humility is the basis for God's relationship with the Hebrew people. In a hymn of gratitude, the psalmist prays, "I bow low before your holy temple/.... The Lord is on high, but cares for the lowly,/and knows the proud from afar" (Ps 138:2, 6). Bowing before God symbolically acknowledges one's inferiority in relation to God.

In the Old Testament, God consistently chooses the insignificant and lowly to further his plan of salvation. First, the humble nomad Abraham was called to be the father of God's chosen people. Then David, a mere shepherd boy in whom his father saw no promise, was chosen by God to head a dynasty that would eventually come to fruition in Christ. In the New Testament, Mary, a young maiden from the despised town of Nazareth in Galilee, was chosen for the greatest privilege ever proffered a human being—that of being the mother of God. In Mary's Canticle of Praise, she recalls her lowliness and proclaims that God "has put down the mighty from their thrones, and exalted those of low degree" (Luke 1:53). Jesus states that the proud who exalt themselves shall be made lowly, and the lowly, on the other hand, will be exalted (Matt 23:12).

The hymn in Philippians 2:5–11 witnesses to the early Christians' conviction that God's Son took on total human abasement, suffered death, and in the end was exalted as Lord. This hymn is often referred to today as the *kenotic hymn,* a term derived from the Greek word, *kenosis,* which means "empty." The term as it is used in the hymn describes the humility of Jesus Christ in emptying himself, clothing himself with our humanity and giving himself to and for us.

Only when a person acquires the humble attitude of Christ can one edify and build up the church in Christ. Thus Paul exhorts the Philippians: "Count others better than yourselves" (Phil 2:3). Humility predisposes one to grasp, insofar as is possible for human beings, the greatness of God and God's attributes of fidelity and love for us. Pride, on the other hand, estranges a person from God because within the proud person's heart, there resides a sense of superiority in relation to other people and engenders doubt that God can do what seems impossible. Thus, a proud person puts up barriers to an intimate relationship with God.

The attitude of deflecting glory from self to God is reflected in Christ's own self-understanding. He looked not to his own good and glory, but rather he placed the salvation of humanity before all else. That was his Father's will, and because his focus was not on himself, he could correctly discern the will of the Father.

Philippians 2:5 introduces the hymn with an exhortation to "have this mind among you, which is yours in Christ Jesus" (Phil 2:5). All that follows in the hymn (Phil 2:6–11) about Jesus, the Lord, is to be the mindset of the Philippians.

The hymn is the story of our salvation, and it sets forth the Jesus Christ as a model for every baptized Christian. Philippians 2:6–8 describes our divine Lord's humiliation in taking on our human nature. In that sense, he was like Adam, but unlike Adam, Jesus did not consider being like God or being equal to God something that he would cling to in spite of the Father's will that he take on our humanity. In obedience and humility, then, he took on the form of a slave and accepted death on the cross. He became the most debased of all creatures that he might serve the Father's will in the plan of our redemption. In this way, Jesus made himself poor (a human among humans) that we might become rich by virtue of his poverty.

The result of Jesus' obedience was his glorification. God raised him and gave him the name "Lord," which is the translation of *Yahweh*. In his place of glory, he receives the homage of Lord, equality with God, the very thing of which he emptied himself for our salvation. As Gordon Fee states: "[I]n Pauline ethics, the principle is love, the pattern is Christ, the power is the Spirit, and their ultimate purpose the glory of God—all of which has been provided for in the death and resurrection of Christ."[72]

"JESUS CHRIST IS LORD!" Hence the church continues to praise and bend the knee to the one who lost all dignity, even his life, that we might share eternal life with him forever.

For Reflection

1. What do Paul's words, "To live is Christ" mean to you? Is there anything in your life that occupies the center of your thoughts, your very life?
2. Think a minute about the possibility of your own death. What do you think of Paul's attitude that death is gain? Think about the possibility of frequent reception of the sacrament of penance. Find out what times are available for confession in your parish, and make plans for receiving this sacrament of God's mercy.
3. What do you think accounts for the negative attitude in contemporary society toward humility and those who are humble?

A Prayer Based on a Sermon
St. Leo the Great: Pope (d. A.D. 461)

LORD,
> help me to remember my dignity,
> and now that I share in God's own nature,
> let me not return by sin to my former base condition.
Let me never forget
> that I have been rescued from the power of darkness
> and brought into the light of God's kingdom.
In Baptism, I became a temple of the Holy Spirit.
Let me never drive away so great a guest by evil conduct
> and become again a slave to the devil,
> for my liberty was bought by the blood of Christ.
This I ask in the name of Jesus,
> my Lord and God. Amen.[73]

III. Sojourners on Earth

Preparation: Read Philippians 3:1 through 4:9 in which Paul warns the Philippians against false teachers and reminds them of the transitory nature of life in this world. Their citizenship is in heaven, not in this world.

> For many, as I have often told you and now tell you even in tears, conduct themselves as enemies of the cross of Christ.... Their minds are occupied with earthly things. But our citizenship is in heaven, and from it we also await a savior, the Lord Jesus Christ. He will change our lowly body to conform with his glorified body by the power that enables him also to bring all things into subjection to himself. (Phil 3:18–21; NAB)

Because of his love for the Philippians, Paul wanted them to live as true Christians who would share with him the joy of being with the Lord. But to share the joys of eternal happiness, they would have to live as citizens not of this world, but rather as citizens of heaven: "Our citizenship *(politeuma),*" he tells them, "is in heaven" (Phil 3:20). The Greek word for *citizenship, politeuma,* was frequently used "to designate a colony of foreigners...whose purpose was to secure the conquered country for the conquering nation by spreading abroad that nation's way of doing things—its customs, its culture, its laws and so on."[74]

To comprehend Paul's exhortation, it is important to remember that by the time Paul wrote his letters, the Roman Empire had conquered the whole Mediterranean world, including northeastern Greece where Philippi was located. Rome sent some of its citizens to make their home in the major cities of the conquered areas. These citizens were at the service of Rome. They were to live the Roman culture in the foreign land, spread the values of the empire and make its values appealing to the conquered peoples. In addition, they were to bring the native peoples to acknowledge the sovereignty of Rome.[75]

By reminding the Philippians that their citizenship is in heaven, Paul is urging them to bring the values of Christ to the people around them. They are to keep in mind that in spite of the difficulties brought upon them as a result of spreading the gospel, they have a lasting home in heaven with the Lord. As sojourners in this world, their job as Christians is to bring others around them to acknowledge the sovereignty of the Lord Jesus.

Paul considered the Philippians to be "partners" with him in the gospel. They had suffered as Paul had suffered for the sake of their belief in Christ: "For to you has been granted, for the sake of Christ, not only to believe in him but also to suffer for him. Yours is the same struggle as you saw in me and now hear about me" (Phil 1:29–30; NAB). Moreover, they had supported Paul when he left Macedonia. In fact, the Philippians had become his pride and joy as expressed in his letter to them. He refers to them as those "...whom I love and long for, my joy and crown." (Phil 4:1).

Unity was to be the essential characteristic for this church that Paul held in his heart with such great affection: "[C]omplete my joy by being of the same mind, with the same love, united in heart, thinking one thing" (Phil 2:2; NAB). The Greek word for "mind" or "mindset" *(phronein),* which Paul used in this passage, refers to a "determined behavior;"[76] that is, the Philippians are to have a mindset like that of Christ whose love and compassion embraced all people and which was obvious in his actions.

Paul reminds the people of the importance of remaining steadfast in the faith. He urges them to struggle "together for the faith of the gospel, not intimidated in any way by...opponents" (Phil 2:7b–28). The notion of a church community struggling together for the faith was just as necessary in the first century as it is today. Frequently, the struggle involved people from outside the community who proclaimed a distorted version of the gospel. In face of that confusion, the early Christians had to hold on to the "deposit of faith" that Paul had left them. In addition, suffering came from their Jewish acquaintances who challenged, taunted and at times turned them over to the Romans as troublemakers. Imprisonment for claiming the name "Christian" was not uncommon. A community who "struggled together" had a better chance of maintaining the true teachings of their beloved Paul than if they faced these tribulations alone.

For Reflection

1. Have you ever experienced feeling like a pariah at your work site because you took a virtuous stand or expressed an opinion that was true to your Catholic faith?
2. What are the values and virtues most difficult for you to witness to in your daily life?
3. Reflect a few minutes on Paul's statement that our "citizenship is in heaven." What are some of life's difficulties that seem less significant or less consequential in view of this fact?

Prayer to Work for the Things We Pray for
St. Thomas More: Statesman and Martyr (d. A.D. 1535)

O LORD,
> give us a mind that is humble
>> quiet, peaceable, patient, and charitable,
>> and a taste of your Holy Spirit
>>> in our thoughts, words, and deeds.

O LORD,
> Give us a lively faith,
>> a firm hope, a fervent charity, a love of you.
> Take from us all lukewarmness in meditation
>> and dullness of prayer.

Give us fervor
  and delight in thinking
  of you, your grace, and your tender compassion
    toward us.
Give us, good Lord, the grace to work for
  the things we pray for. Amen.[77]

Summary of the Main Points in the Letter to the Philippians

Paul had a loving relationship with the Philippians. As he writes to them from prison, he contemplates the possibility of death, which he finds equally acceptable as life because both would give God glory. Paul exhorts the Philippians to maintain unity among themselves. To accomplish this, they must be humble as was Christ, their model. Just as the Lord did not consider his exalted state of divinity something to which he would cling, so too the Philippians are exhorted to humble service of one another. As citizens of heaven, they are to live as sojourners on this earth and spread the values of the kingdom of God.

FOR FURTHER READING

Bloomquist, L. G. *The Function of Suffering in Philippians.* JSNT Sup 78. Sheffield: JSOT, 1993.

Brown, Raymond E. *An Introduction to the New Testament.* Anchor Bible Reference Library. New York: Doubleday, 1997, pp. 483–501.

Byrne, S.J., Brendan. "The Letter to the Philippians," in *The New Jerome Biblical Commentary.* Raymond E. Brown et al, eds. Englewood Cliffs, NJ: Prentice Hall, 1990, pp. 791–97.

"Philippians—Reading Guide," *The Catholic Study Bible. The New American Bible.* New York: Oxford University Press, 1990, pp. RG 514–18.

Letter to the Romans

INTRODUCTION

*T*he Letter to the Romans differs from the other letters that
Paul wrote to the churches. He was not the founder of the
Roman Church, nor had he ever visited it. The letter, however,
specifically indicates Paul's intention to visit this church community in the near future: "I mention you in my prayers, asking
that somehow by God's will I may now at last succeed in coming to you. For I long to see you, that I may impart to you some
spiritual gift to strengthen you" (Rom 1:9b–11).

One thing that the Romans and Paul had in common was
their background in the Graeco-Roman culture. Even though
Paul was a Jew, he had been born in the diaspora (i.e., outside
Palestine) in Tarsus in the area of Cilicia (modern-day Turkey),
and hence the apostle enjoyed Roman citizenship.

Of course, Paul has no postmark on his letter, so an exact dat-
ing is impossible. Because he had already established churches
throughout the area north of the Mediterranean Sea, he most
likely wrote this letter around A.D. 55 or 56. Neither does Paul
have a return address on the letter, but most scholars believe he
wrote it from Corinth on his last visit there. One clue is that
Phoebe, the person carrying the letter, is in Cenchreae, a port city
near Corinth (Rom 16:1). We know that Paul spent significant

time in Corinth, so his statement that he is finished with the work "in these regions" (Rom 15:23), in addition to his mention of Cenchreae, seems to indicate the location of the letter's origin.

Why then did Paul write to the Roman Christians, given the fact that he did not found the Roman Church? From the contents of his letter, two things stand out. First, the churches in Macedonia and Achia had contributed to Paul's collection for the poor in Jerusalem, and he wants the Romans also to play a role in his missionary work by preparing the way for his journey to Jerusalem to deliver the collection. Perhaps many Jews in Jerusalem had gotten wind of the way Paul spoke of the law in his Letter to the Galatians. Hence they might consider it a duty to destroy one who diminished the importance of the Torah. By presenting the body of his teaching in one letter to the Romans, a church that had many Gentile converts, he would nourish their fervor in the faith, and they would no longer be forced by ignorance to stand by quietly while Paul was maligned. Jewish Christians in Rome could be witnesses to his orthodox beliefs and thus verify that he had no intention of destroying the law. In effect, they would be the buffer between Paul and the Jerusalem Jews when he goes there. They could increase Paul's chances for safety as well as demonstrate their willing acceptance of the collection he was waiting to deliver: "When therefore I have completed this, and have delivered to them what has been raised, I shall go on by way of you to Spain" (Rom 15:28). Acceptance of the collection by the Jerusalem Church was of great importance to Paul because it would signify that the churches he had founded among the Gentiles were one in union with the Jewish Christian Church in Jerusalem. Moreover, it was through the Jews that the gospel had become known to the Gentiles. Gentiles therefore were indebted to the Jews, for if they "have come to share in their spiritual blessings, they ought also to be of service to them in material blessings" (Rom 15:27).

A second reason for writing the letter may have been Paul's desire to have their moral and financial support as he turned his face to Spain. His missionary efforts in the northern Mediterranean world had been blessed, and now he prepares the way to go west with the message of salvation of all peoples, Gentiles as well as Jews:

> [S]ince I no longer have any room for work in these regions, and since I have longed for many years to come to you, I hope to see you in passing as I go to Spain, and to be sped on my journey there by you, once I have enjoyed your company for a little. At present, however, I am going to Jerusalem with aid for the saints. (Rom 15:23–25)

Moreover, Paul had friends in the Roman Church. He first met some of them in Corinth following their expulsion from Rome by Emperor Claudius in A.D. 49. Under a decree of Nero after the death of Claudius in A.D. 54, they had returned to Rome. Paul sends greetings to many of them in the last chapter of Romans. Two of them, Prisca and Aquila, had worked with Paul in spreading the gospel. There is no retrievable evidence to verify how the faith reached the large Jewish colony in Rome, but clearly Christianity had put down its roots in the capital city. Probably through the evangelizing efforts of these Jewish Christians, there were Gentile converts in the church community as well.

There are similarities between the Letter to the Galatians and the Letter to the Romans. The major likeness is that both letters treat of our salvation as justification through faith in Jesus Christ, but each letter expresses in its own particular tone the role of the Mosaic Law.

Outline of the Letter to the Romans

Introduction; Greeting, Thanksgiving and Future Plans
(Rom 1:1–17)
  I. Justification: a Gift for All through Faith (Rom 1:18–
    4:25)
  II. The Great Price of God's Love (Rom 5:1–21)
  III. Life in the Spirit (Rom 6:1–8:39)
  IV. Israel's Disbelief (Rom 9:1–11:36)
  V. Requirements of the Christian Life (Rom
    12:1–15:13)
Conclusions (Rom 15:14–16:27)

I. The Gospel Is Power

Preparation: Read Romans 1:1 through 1:17. After the conventional address, greeting and thanksgiving, Paul sets forth in a nutshell the doctrine that the entire letter will elucidate.

> For I am not ashamed of the gospel; it is the power of God for salvation to everyone who has faith, to the Jew first and also to the Greek. For in it the righteousness of God is revealed through faith for faith; as it is written, "He who through faith is righteous shall live." (Rom 1:16–17)

In this short passage, the overall message of the Letter to the Romans is summarized. God, in his righteousness, makes justification and salvation possible for all—Jews and Gentiles alike.

To comprehend better the meaning of *gospel* for Paul, it is helpful to look at its use in the Old Testament. Frequently, *good news* or *gospel* refers to the liberation of God's people from domination under foreign rule. *Good news* also indicates freedom from sin as we see in the later chapters of Isaiah 40–66. Isaiah presents God's saving act on behalf of Israel as "good news," and it was "good news" to be heralded from the mountaintops.

> Go up onto a high mountain,
>   Zion, herald of glad tidings;
> Cry out at the top of your voice
>   Jerusalem, herald of good news!…
> Here comes with power
>   the Lord GOD,…
> Like a shepherd he feeds his flock;
>   in his arms he gathers the lambs,
> Carrying them in his bosom,
>   and leading the ewes with care. (Isa 40:9–11; NAB)

In his conversion experience, Paul came to realize that this good news that Isaiah spoke of so long ago was brought to fulfillment in Christ Jesus. The word *gospel (euangelion)* refers to that which God effected on earth by the death and resurrection of the Lord. Paul's vocation was to be a herald of the gospel to the Gentiles.[78]

In this first statement following the greeting and self-identification, Paul emphasizes that he is not "ashamed of the gospel." Why did Paul think it necessary to make this point? Generally, things that shame a person are those events in life that are scandalous. Because the gospel of Jesus brings news of everything that is good or that has any significance for eternity, where then is there possibility for shame?

The word *scandal* (in Greek *skandalon*), used later by Paul in Romans 11:9 (see also 1 Cor 1:23), is helpful in understanding Paul's negation of shame. A *skandalon* refers to an obstacle, such as a stone, that causes a person to fall. In Paul's letters, it refers to the cross because the cross caused many people to refuse or to lose faith in Jesus.

Even though Jesus brought salvation, which was a long-awaited event in the Old Testament, he was a stumbling block to many Jews as well as to Gentiles who did not believe. That is why Paul maintains that he preaches "Christ crucified, a stumbling block to the Jews and folly to the Gentiles" (1 Cor 1:23). That God would act in and through Jesus who was crucified was unthinkable to many people. Jewish wisdom could not reconcile crucifixion with the notion of a savior or a messiah. Anyone who was hanged on a tree was cursed by God as stated in the book of Deuteronomy: "God's curse rests on him who hangs on a tree" (Deut 21:23; NAB).

In the Greek mind, power could not be reconciled with the absurdity of suffering either, nor could the powerlessness of one hanging on a cross impress one who did not have faith. The scandal of the gospel, then, is that the Son of God suffered death on a cross and that this is an intrinsic part of the good news of our salvation. "[God]...did not spare his own Son but gave him up for us all" (Rom 8:32). For those who reject suffering as part of the Christian life, this fact of faith places God in the realm of the absurd.

In spite of the possibility that Christ's death and resurrection would be rejected by many of his hearers, Paul is not ashamed of the perceived contradictions and the stumbling block this mystery of love presents. Thus, Paul always faces the possibility of persecution as a preacher of foolishness to the Gentiles (who could not conceive of the idea of a god who would die) as well as the majority of Jews (who saw it all as a contradiction to their traditions).

By the time of the writing of the Letter to the Romans, Paul had almost lost his life on more than one occasion because of his testimony to the gospel. He had been chased out of Thessalonica, imprisoned in Philippi and rejected by many Jews and Gentiles alike. Yet, Paul is still able to stand proud in the proclamation of the gospel of the renewed relationship with God that was made possible by the death and resurrection of Jesus Christ. One of Paul's understandings of his mission to spread the gospel to the Gentiles was that it was an act of "worship": "For God is my witness, whom I serve [in Greek, *latreuo,* literally "worship"] with my spirit in the gospel of his Son" (Rom 1:9). Again, when speaking of his ministry to the Gentiles, Paul refers to it as "a priestly service...so that the offering of the Gentiles may be acceptable" (Rom 15:16). Thus it seems that the apostle's understanding of spreading the gospel was that it was so profound and holy that he could refer to it as a form of worship and priestly service.

In spite of all its weak appearance, the gospel is the power of God. Wherever it is proclaimed, God's saving power is present and at work. Because it is the power of God, and not just human proclamation, it can break through to the hearts of the most hardened of sinners, just as the risen Christ broke through the chains of death. Salvation through the death and resurrection of Jesus Christ was for everyone who believed, for the "Jew" (that is, the chosen people with whom God had bound himself in covenant) as well as for the "Greek" (that is, the non-Jew). In the gospel, God has revealed the mystery of all mysteries, which is accessible to everyone through faith.

Paul cites the prophet Habakkuk who spoke of Yahweh's fidelity to Judah in the nation's struggle against the Chaldeans: "The one who through faith is righteous shall live" (Rom 1:17). Judah's faith and trust in God was similar to that of the believer—the one who has faith in Jesus Christ is delivered from the power of eternal death.[79]

For Reflection

1. Is the gospel still a scandal today? How has that been demon-strated in your experience?
2. The power of the gospel is that which is proclaimed each time we hear the word of God at Mass. Do you have the opportunity to proclaim the word? Is it something special to you?
3. What does it mean to you "to live in faith"?

Prayer of Gratitude for God's Goodness to Us Sinners
St. Gregory of Nyssa: Priest, Doctor of the Church (d. 394)

> LORD,
> from you flows true and continual kindness.
> You had cast us off and justly so,
> but in your mercy you forgave.
> You were at odds with us,
> and you reconciled us.
> You had set a curse on us,
> and you blessed us.
> You had banished us from the garden,
> and you called us back again.
> You took away the fig leaves
> that had been an unsuitable garment,
> and you clothed us in a cloak of great value.
> You flung wide the prison gates,
> and you gave the condemned a pardon.
> You sprinkled clean water on us,
> and you washed away the dirt. Amen.[80]

II. A Gift for All through Faith

Preparation: Read Romans 1:18 through 4:25 in which Paul explains that the broken relationship with God, which came about with sin, is rectified by Christ's death and resurrection as a gift and not by human effort.

> [T]he righteousness of God has been manifested apart from law, although the law and the prophets bear witness to it, the righteousness of God through faith in Jesus Christ for all who believe. For there is no distinction; since all have sinned and fall short of the glory of God, they are justified by his grace as a gift, through the redemption which is in Christ Jesus, whom God put forward as an expiation by his blood, to be received by faith. This was to show God's righteousness, because in his divine forbearance he had passed over former sins; it was to prove at the present time that he himself is righteous and that he justifies him who has faith in Jesus. (Rom 3:21–26)

In Romans 1:18 to 3:20, Paul set the stage for this passage. All have sinned, whether Gentile or Jew. Though the Gentiles did not have the Mosaic Law, they could have known God from the very message of nature. Instead, in their arrogance, they used nature in making for themselves false images to worship. Thus, they ignored the revelation of the Creator through the medium of nature, and so God gave them over to their sinfulness, which reached its depths in moral perversion—sexual and homosexual activities as well as a catalogue of other vices (Rom 1:18–32).

But Paul points out that the Gentiles are not alone in their sinfulness. The Jews too have sinned, even though they have the Law of Moses to indicate for them the path of fidelity to God.

They have usurped God's role by standing in judgment of the Gentiles, all the while knowing that judgment belongs to God alone (Rom 2:1–3). The Jews, who had superior moral knowledge because of the Law, sinned all the same. They flaunted God's patience and kindness and failed to repent. They refused to turn their hearts to God, thus making their circumcision uncircumcision (Rom 2:25–29). Paul states that the privileged status of the people of God through the covenant becomes null and void without righteous living. Circumcision does not guarantee salvation. The Jews' uncircumcision of heart (i.e., refusal to repent) has thereby subjected them to the judgment of God on the last day (Rom 2:4–5). Thus the Gentiles who sinned without the Law as well as the Jews who sinned under the Law are subject to God's wrath (Rom 2:4–11). Paul points to scripture as witness to this universal sinfulness (Rom 3:10–11).

Now that Paul has pointed out what happens to all humanity without the gospel, he explains in Romans 3:21–26 that God graciously offers everyone who has faith in Jesus Christ a new relationship with God. Basically, that is the content of the gospel or good news.

Paul is moving his readers from the idea of the old eon under the Law to the new eon under the gospel, that is, to the eschatological age or end-time initiated by Jesus. In this new age, God's saving power is available to everyone, not to Israel alone, and it is graciously offered to all through faith.

Paul uses four ways to explain the effects of the death and resurrection of Jesus: "justification, redemption, expiation and pardon of sins."[81] The first three are less familiar to us today. The word *justification* (in Greek, *dikaiosyne*) explains the restored human relationship with God. This restoration of our relationship with God came through the death and resurrection of Jesus. To use a metaphor from the court of law, St. Paul maintains that all people stand guilty before God (Rom 3:23). According to God's plan to save us, however, Christ stepped forward, as it were, and took on our guilt. He took our place as the one deserving of death, and hence we have been acquitted, that is, we have been "justified" *(dikaioumene)*. Our relationship with God has been restored. How? We are justified through our "redemption that comes through Jesus Christ" (Rom 3:24). That introduces the reader to another effect of the Christ event.

As a second metaphor, Paul makes use of the word *redemption (apolytrosis)* to indicate what Christ's death and resurrection did for us in regard to our enslavement under sin. As the Israelites were ransomed from captivity in Egypt (LXX,[82] Ps 78:35),[83] so also were we ransomed from our enslavement to sin. The notion of Jesus as our "redemption" brings out the price of our sins. *Redemption* in the secular world of Paul had to do with buying back a slave. Hence, Paul adapted this terminology to express what God did for us in Jesus. Humanity had fallen into the slavery of sin. Sin had become the master; the sinner was its servant, wholly unable to free himself or herself. From this condition, humanity was redeemed with the price of Jesus' own life.

The apostle uses a third metaphor in Rom 3:25, that of God putting Jesus Christ forward as an "expiation" or "a means of expiation" *(hilasterion)* for our sins. The word *expiation* relates Jesus' self-sacrifice for us to the Day of Atonement sacrifice in the Old Testament (see Exod 25:17–22; Lev 23:26–31). Once a year, the High Priest entered the Holy of Holies and sprinkled the blood of an animal on the "mercy seat" (in Greek, *hilasterion*). That act was the means that God had given Israel through which he would forgive their sins. Analogous to that imagery and in place of that atonement sacrifice, Jesus, through his death on the cross, became both the "mercy seat" *(hilasterion)* and the blood required for the sprinkling of the *hilasterion*. In other words, Jesus, through the shedding of his blood, replaced the Old Testament means of expiating the sins of the people through the blood of animals. Thus, Christ is depicted "as the new 'mercy seat,' presented or displayed by the Father as a means of expiating or wiping away the sins of humanity."[84]

The metaphor "passing over" our sins stresses that the debt incurred by past sins (i.e., the honor not given God because of sin) has been canceled. "It is, however, still another manifestation of grace that God has granted me, for he has not only created, justified, and redeemed me, but he has wrought all this."[85]

All this is God's gift to us through faith. Paul points to the prophet Habakkuk who noted, "The one who is just shall find life through faith" (Hab 2:4 [my translation]). (As the letter progresses, Paul will show that works are a response to this gift. They express the freedom given each human being by God to accept or reject the gift). God's offer of an intimate relationship with us is accessible through faith, Paul explains (Rom 3:22). Faith, as expressed in the Pauline letters, is a personal commitment to God to accept all that has been revealed through Jesus Christ. Faith is a commitment that encompasses total dependence on God and God's action in the world as well as in one's own life. As Fr. Brendan Byrne, S.J., so aptly states: "The justification that ensues is entirely the work of God but, on the human side, faith is the vehicle of its operation. Through faith God is able to draw sinful human beings into the scope of divine righteousness displayed in the obedient death of Christ."[86]

In Chapter 4 of Romans, Paul gives a concrete example of the point he was presenting in Romans 3:21–26. By means of the scriptural account of Abraham in Genesis 15–17, he sets forth God's word as an affirmation of his teaching on justification by faith rather than by human effort. Thus, he illustrates his position that justification is God's gift, not something that human beings can merit by obeying the law.

By turning to Abraham as a model of one justified by faith, Paul is taking a position contrary to that of his contemporary Jews. Their position maintained that Abraham anticipated the law by obeying God's injunction concerning circumcision and by passing the test of obedience regarding his son, Isaac. This view is clearly expressed by Ben Sira: "He [Abraham] kept the law of the Most high, and entered into a covenant with him; he certified the covenant in his flesh and when he was tested he proved faithful" (Sir 44:20; NRSV). "His faithfulness under test (Gen 22:1–18) and even his act of faith (Gen 15:6) could be understood as a meritorious act that won blessings for all his descendants."[87] But Paul uses the same Old Testament figure to illustrate that from a purely human perspective, God's promise of progeny to Abraham was an impossible feat given the fact that Sarah was barren. Nevertheless, Abraham put his trust in God's promise, and he was justified because of his faith, not because of the Law because the Law did not exist until given to Moses some four or five centuries later.

For Reflection

1. Try to verbalize your understanding of justification (as God's free gift to us) to a spouse, friend or colleague. What role do good works play?
2. Pope John Paul II, in the encyclical letter, "Mission of the Redeemer," *("Redemptoris Missio")* states: "The universal call to holiness is closely linked to the universal call to mission. Every member of the faithful is called to holiness and to mission" (# 90). Many people think holiness is beyond their reach because our baptismal innocence (our justification) is frequently lost. What is your view of being holy, and do you really want to be a holy person? Why or why not?

The Christopher Prayer
Father James Keller, M.M.: Founder of the Christophers

FATHER,
   grant that I may be a bearer of Christ Jesus, Your Son.
   Allow me to warm the often cold, impersonal scene
      of modern life
      with Your burning love.
   Strengthen me, by Your Holy Spirit,
      to carry out my mission of changing the world
      or some definite part of it for the better.
   Despite my lamentable failures,
      bring home to me that my advantages
      are Your blessings to be shared with others.
   Make me more energetic in setting to rights
      what I find wrong with the world
      instead of complaining about it or myself.
   Nourish in me a practical desire
      to build up rather than tear down,
      to reconcile more than polarize,
      to go out on a limb rather than crave security.
   Never let me forget
      that it is far better to light one candle
      than to curse the darkness.
      And to join my light, one day, with Yours. Amen.[88]

III. The Fruits of Justification

Preparation: Read Romans 5:1 through 5:21. In this section, Paul moves from the explanation of justification by faith to a focus on God's love. Hence, we move into a less juridical portion of the letter than the former chapters of Romans.

Since we are justified by faith, we have peace with God through our Lord Jesus Christ. Through him we have obtained access to this grace in which we stand, and we rejoice in our hope of sharing the glory of God. More than that, we rejoice in our sufferings, knowing that suffering produces endurance, and endurance produces character, and character produces hope, and hope does not disappoint us, because God's love has been poured into our hearts through the Holy Spirit which has been given to us. While we were still weak, at the right time Christ died for the ungodly.... God shows his love for us in that while we were yet sinners Christ died for us. Since...we are now justified by his blood, much more shall we be saved by him from the wrath of God. For if while we were enemies we were reconciled to God by the death of his Son, much more, now that we are reconciled, shall we be saved by his life.... [W]e also rejoice in God through our Lord Jesus Christ, through whom we have now received our reconciliation. (Rom 5:1–11)

Now that St. Paul has set forth his exposition of God's justification and how it was achieved by Christ on our behalf, he begins his treatise on Christian life, as the channel through which God's gift of justification is accepted and maintained. As a result of God's justification, humanity is at peace with God. *Peace (eirene)* has the sense of the Old Testament *shalom,* "the fullness of right relationship that is implied in justification itself."[89] Once estranged from God, we are now able to experience the peace that accompanies this reconciliation. Human beings can now enjoy a "peace with God through our Lord Jesus Christ" (Rom 5:1). The peace of which Paul speaks in Romans 5:1 flows from the fact that humanity is no longer under the burden of God's wrath. Through his death, Christ changed God's wrath to God's peace.

As Christians, we also have the hope of sharing God's glory (Rom 5:2) in the fullness of the kingdom of God. Before God's gift of justification was made accessible to us through faith in Jesus Christ, there was no basis for hope of standing confidently before God in an atmosphere of grace. To the contrary, humanity deserved God's wrath, and there was no path of salvation open by which people could hope for it: "For the wrath of God is revealed from heaven against all ungodliness and wickedness of human beings who by their wickedness suppress the truth" (Rom 1:18).

Justification, however, transformed that hopeless scenario. God intervened and provided a way that gives all human beings "hope of sharing the glory of God" (Rom 5:2). God, through Christ, redeemed us, expiated our sins and forgave the debt we owed, thereby reconciling us to God and making our salvation possible.

All these metaphors focus on God's great love for all people. It is this good news, the gospel, that gives us hope for a new future at the end-time. This new future has already begun in the sense that baptized persons enjoy an intimate relationship with God. They already share God's life (Rom 1:2), which was not possible from the time of Adam's fall up to the time of Jesus' death and resurrection. The new life that Christ gained for us is not yet in its fullness, a completion that will characterize the end-time. Our new present status in relation to God was not our own achievement, but that which was brought about by Christ, God's Son, who gave his life for us on the cross (Rom 5:6).

Paul instructs his readers concerning the value of suffering: "Suffering produces endurance, endurance produces character, and character produces hope" (Rom 5:3). With the grace that Christ's death and resurrection brought, afflictions can not only be endured, but they can actually promote endurance or steadfastness in the Christian. That being so, he or she can continue living a life of grace in this world regardless of those events or things in life that might be a "stumbling block" were it not for God's grace.[90]

Endurance, in turn, produces character. *Character* is the translation of a Greek word, *dokime,* which indicates something that has been tried and tested, as in those who have been persecuted or harassed because of their faith. Character then produces hope in one who has been sustained by grace through testing in tribulation. Hope keeps the baptized person focused on the future in which God manifests our salvation in its fullness. It is in that sense that the gospel holds out a new future for the baptized person. Justification then initiates a moral life in harmony with one's vocation as a Christian.

Suffering has this positive chainlike effect because it has been redeemed by Christ's own sufferings. Later in the letter, Paul maintains that as Christians, we suffer "with Christ" (Rom 8:18). Sufferings are part of our heritage as "children of God and co-heirs with Christ, provided we suffer with him in order that we may be glorified with him." For those who have been justified by Christ through his suffering and death on the cross, afflictions, hardships and troubles are part of the present time. As such, they remind us that this new life we already experience is only a "down payment" (2 Cor 1:22) of the fullness of life that is yet to come.

God's love, Paul maintains, "has been poured into our hearts through the Holy Spirit" (Rom 5:5). The sense of God "pouring" love into our hearts is another illustration of the giftedness of our justification. Because this love originates with God, it is totally gratuitous and comes to us by the Holy Spirit so that the Christian can be certain of its authenticity. This experience of God's love in this world, "the first fruits of the Spirit," sustains the Christian's hope for the full manifestation of God's love for all eternity.

In Romans 5:6–11, Paul explains how this love for us has been concretely expressed. As part of the world's unredeemed wickedness, we deserved God's wrath. But God chose as it were to ignore the scales of justice and reconciled us to himself through the death of his son. Such a gift was inconceivable, Paul maintains (Rom 5:6–11), because it was given while we were still God's enemies, that is, while we were "godless" (*asebos,* "without reverence for God").[91] Our relationship with God, broken by sin and human arrogance, was restored, but it was restored at a great price, the death of his Son.

In Romans 5:12–21, Paul sets Christ and the power of his gift of justification over against the power of Adam and sin. Adam's sin had introduced death into the world; Christ's death and resurrection brought the possibility of eternal life.

For Reflection

1. What meaning does St. Paul attribute to the Christians' sufferings or afflictions?
2. Is it difficult for you to accept that God could love you as an individual so much as to give his only beloved son for your salvation?
3. Take some time alone to contemplate God's great love for you.

From St. Augustine's Soliloquies (1, I, 5)
St. Augustine: Bishop, Doctor of the Church (d. A.D. 430)

Receive me, I pray,…most merciful Father,
me your fugitive!
Receive me, your household servant,
fleeing from my delusions,
which took me in, though I was a stranger,
fleeing from you.…
Teach me how to come to you…
How to make my way to you I do not know.
Tell me how; make it plain;
equip me for the journey!

Increase my faith,
increase my hope,
increase my charity,
O Goodness unique and admirable.[92]

IV. Death and Sin Are Rendered Helpless

Preparation: Read Romans 6:1 through 8:39. In this section, the apostle presents baptism as the means of freedom from sin and death and demonstrates that life lived according to the Spirit is the only acceptable response to God's gift of justification.

> What shall we say then? Are we to continue to sin that grace may abound? By no means! How can we who died to sin still live in it? Do you not know that all of us who have been baptized into Christ Jesus were baptized into his death? We are buried therefore with him by baptism into death, so that as Christ was raised from the dead by the glory of the Father, we too might walk in newness of life. For as we have been united with him in a death like his, we shall be united with him in a resurrection like his. We know that our old self was crucified with him so that the sinful body might be destroyed, and we might no longer be enslaved to sin. For he who has died is freed from sin. But if we have died with Christ, we believe that we shall also live with him. For we know that Christ being raised from the dead will never die again; death no longer has dominion over him. The death he died he died to sin, once for all, but the life he lives he lives to God. So you also must consider yourselves dead to sin and alive to God in Christ Jesus. (Rom 6:1–11)

At times in his Letter to the Romans, Paul uses a common first-century rhetorical method of argument in which an expected answer is obvious. At the beginning of this passage, there is one such example wherein Paul dialogues with an imaginary person. Through the mouth of the imaginary partner, Paul poses the objections he believes the church at Rome might make if he were addressing them in person. He then proceeds to respond to the false inferences.

The imaginary dialogue partner poses the question that because the manifestation of God's righteousness is made evident by sin on the part of human beings, would it not follow that sinning would be a good thing? It would give God the opportunity to demonstrate his righteousness by forgiving over and over again (Rom 6:1). Paul's response is emphatic: "By no means!" (Rom 6:2) Such a position is totally illogical. Those who follow Christ have been liberated from the power of sin, so it would be senseless for Christians to allow sin to enslave them again. Slavery to sin ceased with life in Christ through baptism because Christ, by his dying and rising, broke the power of sin, which was most manifest in the power of death. He separated us from sin like death separates us from life. That is what Paul means when he says that we "have been baptized into his [Christ's] death" (Rom 6:3). Together with this break from sin comes death to the old life of sin. No longer is one bound by the cravings to sin because Christ freed us from slavery to sin. Because that power is broken, sin has no potential to assert and impose itself upon the human being.

Not only have we died with Christ, but we have likewise been buried with him in baptism: "Do you not know that all of us who have been baptized into Christ Jesus were baptized into his death?" (Rom 6:3) Burial verifies the certainty of death. "Baptism is the ritual act that portrays this burial."[93]

How a person lives one's life after baptism flows out of one's union with Christ, who acts in baptism to make the Christian one with him. That union with Christ involves a break with sin because sin and Christ's life are totally incompatible. Hence, Paul exhorts the Christian: "Let not sin therefore reign in your mortal bodies" (Rom 6:12). The glory of God was lost to humanity through the sin of Adam: "All have sinned and fall short of the glory of God" (Rom 3:23). Through baptism, the very foundation of what it is to be human in the Christian sense of the word (i.e., the glory of God that was the basis of human dignity before sin) is regained through baptism.

Both death and burial are flagrant reminders of the reality of sin. Early Christian baptismal ritual emphasized and dramatized that actuality. At the time of Paul, the Jewish pools for ritual cleansing were likely to have been used as baptismal pools by Christians. As archaeological digs have revealed, the Jewish immersion baths, called *miqva'ot,* used for purification before offering sacrifice in the temple, had divided steps leading down into the pool. The one to be purified descended on the right side of the steps, immersed in the pool, and ascended on the left side of the steps so as not to incur uncleanness again.[94] This imagery may be reflected in Paul's explanation of baptism as dying with Christ (descending), being buried with him (immersion) and rising with him (ascending).

Paul also explains baptism in terms of the Christian being "united with" Christ in a death like his (Rom 6:5). The Greek word for *united with* is *symphytoi,* a horticulture word that literally means "grafted onto." The imagery of one being "grafted onto" Christ stresses the close union of the baptized person with the Lord. As Christ died, giving up any claim to divinity as a human being, so also the baptized person is crucified, nailed to the cross with Christ and dies to the old life before baptism. Paul's imperative is actually to live the life into which one has been transformed in baptism. In other words: "Become the Christian that you have been enabled to be! You have been co-crucified with Christ; you have died with him to sin!"[95]

Not only is the Christian united with Christ in his death, but the baptized person is also united with him in his resurrection. Those who have been baptized share an intimate life with Christ. As Fr. Fitzmyer states, they "have become grown-together with him."[96] They share the very life of the stock, Christ. No one has a right to this union, but the baptized person is "grafted" in accordance with the gratuitous will of the Lord, who desires to share his life. Thus the baptized person does not have to await a future in which to live this life, but he or she already shares Christ's life in the here and now.[97]

Christ, risen from the dead, is no longer subject to death. The ultimate power of evil is stripped of its potential forever, and now Christians share in this triumph with Christ. The finality of death can never overcome them again. The death and resurrection are at the very heart of the good news of our salvation.

For Reflection

1. God took the initiative in restoring a good relationship with us. In response to and acceptance of this great gift of justification, how do you show your gratitude through love?
2. If we cannot achieve our own salvation by good works, what role do good works have in one's life?
3. What symbol of baptism is most meaningful to you? Why?
4. Water is used to baptize a person. What are the characteristics of water that make it a meaningful symbol?

Prayer for Transformation
St. John Gabriel Perboyre: Missionary and Martyr (d. 1840)

O MY DIVINE SAVIOR,
    transform me into Yourself.
May my hands be the hands of Jesus.
May my tongue be the tongue of Jesus.
Grant that every faculty of my body
    may serve only to glorify You.
Above all,
    transform my soul and all its powers
    so that my memory, will and affections
    may be the memory, will and affections of Jesus.
I pray you to destroy in me
    all that is not of You.
Grant that I may live
    but in You, by You and for You,
    so that I may truly say, with St. Paul,
    "I live—now not I—
    But Christ lives in me!" Amen.[98]

V. LIFE IN THE SPIRIT

Preparation: Read Romans 8:1 through 8:13 in which Paul describes the life of the Spirit in contrast to life under the power of the "flesh."

There is therefore now no condemnation for those who are in Christ Jesus. For the law of the Spirit of life in Christ Jesus has set you free from the law of sin and death....For those who live according to the flesh set their minds on the things of the flesh, but those who live according to the Spirit set their minds on the things of the Spirit. To set the mind on the flesh is death, but to set the mind on the Spirit is life and peace. For the reason the mind that is set on the flesh is hostile to God; it does not submit to God's law—indeed it cannot, and those who are in the flesh cannot please God.

But you are not in the flesh; you are in the Spirit, since the Spirit of God dwells in you. Anyone who does not have the Spirit of Christ does not belong to him. If Christ is in you, though...[I] the body is dead because of sin, the Spirit is life because of righteousness. If the Spirit of him who raised Jesus from the dead dwells in you, he who raised Christ from the dead will give life to your mortal bodies also through his Spirit that dwells in you.

So...we are debtors, not to the flesh, to live according to the flesh—for if you live according to the flesh, you will die; but if by the Spirit you put to death the deeds of the body, you will live. For all who are led by the Spirit of God are children of God. For you did not receive a spirit of slavery to fall back into fear, but you have received a spirit of adoption. When we cry, "Abba! Father!" it is that very Spirit bearing witness with our spirit that we are children of God, and if children, then heirs, heirs of God and joint heirs with Christ—if, in fact, we suffer with him so that we may also be glorified with him.

I consider that the sufferings of this present time are not worth comparing with the glory about to be revealed to us. (Rom 8:1–18; NRSV)

In Romans 6, Paul insisted on moral responsibility as the only appropriate response to the gift of justification. One cannot live a life joined to Christ and at the same time live a life of sin, which is the enemy Christ died to overcome. Baptism empowers a person to live a new life of freedom under God's grace (Rom 7:1–6). Now, in Romans 8, Paul deals with the power of the Spirit by which Christians are enabled to live in a world where the power of the flesh seeks to overcome the power of the Spirit.

The apostle begins this chapter with the assertion that God's judgment has fallen on sin. The power of sin seeks to disorient the baptized from the life of the Spirit in which they enjoy freedom won for them by Jesus Christ. The baptized person has the freedom to submit to Christ or to submit to sin. In baptism, they have been given a new heart, as it were, in fulfillment of God's promise through the prophet Ezekiel: "I will give you a new heart and place a new spirit within you, taking from your bodies your stony hearts and giving you natural hearts" (Ezek 36:26; NAB). Not bound by the bonds of sin, those committed to Christ have not only the freedom to say "no" to the power of sin, but they are empowered by the Spirit to overcome sin and to say "yes" to the Spirit's urgings.

Paul speaks of the "flesh" and the "spirit" in terms of two domains at war with one another. Those who belong to the flesh have as their focus the things of the flesh. The flesh can lead to death alone; the Spirit to final life with Christ at the end-time. Why? Because each has its respective mindset. The flesh seeks its own will, and thus it pits itself against Christ and his Spirit. Those who belong to the realm of the flesh cannot accept obedience to Christ, and thus they refuse the relationship with Christ that he offers us in baptism. They cannot please God, and hence they cannot hope for the peace of one who lives the life of freedom in the Spirit (Rom 8:8). They are "hostile to God," and they are a consistent challenge to the baptized who belong to the realm of the Spirit. Those who adhere to the realm of the Spirit have the mindset of the Spirit (Rom 8:5–7). They see life lived according to the law of God as a means of maintaining God's gift of justification, in which the lost relationship with God was reclaimed by Christ.

Paul acknowledges that the body of the baptized person is still subject to physical death. Bodily mortality is the trace left upon humanity by Adam's sin that no one escapes (Rom 8:10). But in spite of this mortality of the body, "there really is a destiny to eternal life on the basis of the righteousness created by the Spirit.…[R]ighteousness is the passport to salvation, the essential condition for entrance into eternal life."[99] This righteousness is not a personal achievement through righteous living done to merit it but a righteousness that is achieved by the Spirit dwelling in them. The Spirit, Paul says, dwells within the baptized person, and thus the Spirit is "the determining force of their lives."[100] It is the life of the Spirit dwelling within the person that enables the believer to already live the life of the end-time. The Spirit enables them to live according to God's law or, as Paul terms it, the life of the Spirit. That is what Paul means by his statement that the "Spirit means life because of righteousness" (Rom 8:10).

Because we have been "grafted" onto Christ and now live the life of the Spirit, and because Jesus is God's Son, we too are God's children with the same privileges as Jesus. In the Old Testament, the nation of Israel was called God's Son or God's child to emphasize the intimacy of God with the people. With the death and resurrection of Jesus, this privilege became that of the baptized person who, by the Holy Spirit, is united with the risen Christ. Because of our adopted status in relationship to God, we are brothers and sisters of Christ.

Adoption in the Graeco-Roman world transferred the authority of a parent to someone else. A new relationship was established with the adoptive parent, and all ties of the previous parent or authority were broken. The new father assumed authority over the child, and the son responded with assuming the responsibilities and privileges of a naturally born son.

Through the Spirit in baptism, we have been adopted by God. We have inherited all that is Christ's as God's Son. We have the privilege of calling God "Abba," that is, "Father" or "Daddy," for we are not slaves of God (as pagan gods enslaved their devotees) in which we would live in fear and trembling. No, we are God's family; we belong to the household of God. We are God's children who enjoy the status of children and have Jesus as our elder brother. As children of God and brothers and sisters of Jesus Christ, we are summoned by the Spirit dwelling within us to take on the family image.

As children belonging to the family of God, we inherit that which is Christ's by reason of his sonship. Sufferings inflicted on the body of Christ become our sufferings as well—the opposition, the hatred, the persecution from the enemies of God. That is indeed "suffering with him," not a lonely experience of isolation, but a suffering in union with our brother, Jesus Christ.

Whatever our sufferings, they can never be compared with the glory that is to come. Because we are citizens of heaven, this earth is not our home. As foreigners in a land, we cannot expect to be treated as its citizens. The treatment characteristic of our heavenly home is yet to come, and that will be to share in the glory of the risen Christ.

For Reflection

1. What implications does being children of God have for our lives?
2. If we belong to God's family, it is important that we take on the family "image." Are there changes that need to be made in your life to be recognized as a child of God and hence a brother or sister of Jesus?
3. How can you live life in a way that better illustrates that our citizenship is not of this world but of heaven?

Prayer of Self-Offering to God
St. Nicholas of Flue: Saint of Switzerland (d. A.D. 1487)

MY LORD AND MY GOD,
  remove far from me whatever keeps me from you.
My Lord and my God,
  confer upon me whatever enables me to reach you.
My Lord and my God,
  free me from self and make me wholly yours. Amen.[101]

VI. THE GOSPEL AND ISRAEL

Preparation: Read Romans 9 through 12 in which Paul now explains that God, who included the Gentiles in "the community of salvation," maintains his relationship to Israel as his people and will include them also as the divine plan unfolds.

I am speaking the truth in Christ,...I could wish that I myself were accursed and cut off from Christ for the sake of my...kinsmen by race. They are Israelites, and to them belong the sonship, the glory, the covenants, the giving of the law, the worship and the promises; to them belong the patriarchs, and of their race, according to the flesh, is the Christ....But it is not as though the word of God had failed. For not all who are descended from Israel belong to Israel, and not all are children of Abraham because they are his descendants....What if God, desiring to show his wrath and to make known his power, has endured with much patience the vessels of wrath made for destruction, in order to make known the riches of his glory for the vessels of mercy, which he has prepared beforehand for glory?...Gentiles who did not

pursue righteousness have attained it, that is, righteousness through faith...Israel who pursued the
righteousness which is based on law did not succeed
in fulfilling that law....They have stumbled over the
stumbling stone....Has God rejected his people? By
no means!...But through their trespass salvation has
come to the Gentiles, so as to make Israel jeal-
ous....If some of the branches were broken off, and
you, a wild olive shoot, were grafted in their place to
share the richness of the olive tree, do not boast over
the branches. If you do boast, remember it is not you
that support the root, but the root that supports
you....A hardening has come upon part of Israel,
until the full number of the Gentiles come in, and so
all Israel will be saved....Just as you were once disobedient to God but now have received mercy
because of their disobedience, so they have now
been disobedient in order that by the mercy shown
to you, they also may receive mercy. (Rom 9:1–7, 22,
30–32; 11:1, 11, 17, 25, 30)

In Romans 1 through 4, Paul set forth the gospel in terms of
God's inclusion of Jews and Gentiles in his universal salvific plan,
even though both Jews and Gentiles sinned. The apostle now deals
with the issue that the majority of the Jews rejected, that is, God's
offer of justification in Jesus Christ. "Has God 'included' the Gentiles at the terrible cost of 'excluding' the People to whom the
promises were originally entrusted?"[102] Paul sets out to demonstrate that God has not acted contrary to his promises to Israel.

Paul expresses his "sorrow" and "grief" that his "kinsmen by
race" have rejected the gospel: "I could wish that I myself were
accursed and cut off from Christ for the sake of my...kinsmen"
(Rom 9:3). Here he expresses his pain and emotion of sorrow in
terms of Moses' prayer. Moses also grieved over the hardened

hearts of his people: "If you would only forgive their sin! If you will not, then strike me out of the book that you have written" (Exod 32:32; NAB). Essentially, Paul is saying that he would be willing to undergo the worst and most unthinkable of punishments if it would translate into Israel's salvation.[103]

Paul refers to his people as "Israelites," a name assigned to them when God changed Jacob's name to Israel: "You shall no longer be spoken of as Jacob, but as Israel" (Gen 32:29; NAB). The apostle points out seven great privileges of which Israel was very proud. First of all, to them belongs the "sonship"; that is, they were chosen by God and called his "sons," a title that expressed God's tender affection for these people (i.e., Deut 1:31; 8:5; 14:1; Isa 1:2; Wis 2:13; 16:26).[104] Second, they had the glory of God, or the presence of God, among them in the ark and in the cloud while wandering in the desert after their escape from Egypt (i.e., Exod 16:10–12). As children of Abraham, they had the covenants in which God was bound in fidelity to his people, first through Abraham (Gen 15:18), then Isaac (Gen 26:3–5) and finally Moses (Exod 24:7–8). God had given them the Law, their beloved Torah, so that they might know what the will of God was for them and consequently respond in fidelity. Israel also had the cult or worship that differed greatly from pagan forms of worship (i.e., participation in prostitution, the sacrifice of children, etc.). Israel's worship had been legislated by God as the means of honoring him. To Israel also belonged the promises, for example, the promise of a land and many descendants. They also had the patriarchs Abraham, Isaac and Jacob among their ancestors. And last, but certainly not the least, they can boast that the Messiah came from their stock, in spite of the fact that the majority of the Jews did not recognize him.[105]

Does the rejection by the majority of Jews mean that God's word failed? (Rom 9:6). No, Paul explains. God has been faithful to his word. Not all who by birthright call themselves

Israelites and children of Abraham are indeed so. God's promises were to "Israel of faith."[106]

Paul then goes on to suggest that the Gentiles were part of God's plan all along. He refers to them as "vessels of wrath" (Rom 9:22) because of their pagan adherence before they heard the gospel. God used the Gentiles to bring the Jews around to belief in Jesus as God's Son and Messiah. Out of God's mercy, the Gentiles ("the vessels of mercy") who had faith were justified (Rom 9:23). God's patience with Israel, as Fitzmyer explains, endures so that in time they also will be the objects of God's mercy.[107]

Paul points out the irony involved in Jewish and Gentile response to the gospel. The Gentiles, who did not seek to be justified by works of the Law, were justified by faith. The Jews, on the other hand, sought to be justified through observance of the Law (Rom 9:30–31), but, as Paul demonstrated earlier in this letter (Rom 1:1–4:1ff), justification does not occur as a result of good works. Is Paul denigrating the value of good works? To the contrary, he recognizes that good works have always been required in accordance with God's commands (see Rom 5 through 8). The problem for Jews who reject Christ lies in the difficulty of not acknowledging their sinfulness and refusing to rely on God's grace for justification.

For most of the Jews, Christ was a stumbling block. "[T]he 'stone of stumbling' and 'rock of offense' that God 'places' in Israel…is the crucified Messiah, Jesus. The Messiah that God sent to Israel was not a triumphant leader…but one 'put forward' as a hilasterion ['mercy seat'] for sin (3:25)."[108] But Paul makes it clear that their stumbling was no surprise to God; in fact, God had foreseen their stubbornness of heart and foretold it through the prophet Isaiah (28:16): "Behold, I am laying in Zion a stone that will make men stumble, a rock that will make them fall; and he who believes in him will not be put to shame" (Rom 9:33). "Running madly and with zeal in pursuit of a certain kind of uprightness, Israel has failed to see the obstacle….It has failed to acknowledge Christ and the role that Israel has come to play in God's providence for humanity."[109]

Paul's love for his people is profound: "My heart's desire and prayer to God for them is that they may be saved" (Rom 10:1). One might unhesitatingly conclude that God has rejected his people along with the covenants, but that is not Paul's conclusion. They are God's people, and just as in God's mercy Paul was rescued from the mistaken direction of his life, so too does he have confidence that Israel will be awakened from its stupor as well.

St. Paul goes on to use an analogy of tree grafting to clarify the Gentile and Jewish situation (Rom 11:16b–24). The Gentiles are the wild olive branch in the analogy. They were grafted onto the cultivated olive tree (i.e., the patriarchs and all the people of God in the Old Testament) in place of branches that were cut off (i.e., the Israelites who rejected the gospel). Through the root, the Gentiles receive nourishment from the holiness of the Old Testament Jewish people dedicated to God. The goodness of the patriarchs and saintly people in Israel's history fosters the holiness of the Gentiles (Rom 11:17).[110] Therefore, Paul warns the Gentiles that they are not to boast or consider themselves greater than Israel. In so doing, they would demonstrate their lack of understanding of their indebtedness to Israel in sharing the graces of the Christ event (Rom 11:18).

Paul is encouraged by God's plan of salvation. God has made use of Israel's rejection of Jesus and his good news by incorporating Israel's rejection into the plan of salvation of all peoples. Because the people of God refused to accept the gospel, Paul was given the mission to take the gospel to the Gentiles. On seeing that the Gentiles were receiving Israel's inheritance (i.e., being made righteous before God), they themselves would turn and be saved through God's grace (Rom 11:14).

The Jews, Paul maintains, are not ignorant of God. In the previous chapter (Rom 10:2), the apostle testifies that Israel "has a zeal for God, but it is not enlightened." " 'Zeal' for God, his law, or his Temple was considered the characteristic of the faithful Jew....They know God indeed and are devoted to his service, seeking to live in accordance with his will; but they do not recognize that quality in him which really matters....[They are] ignorant of that divine uprightness...which has been revealed in the gospel."[111]

Speaking of Israel that does not accept the gospel of God's mercy based on faith, Paul asserts that "the others, if they do not persist in their unbelief, will be grafted in, for God has the power to graft them in again" (Rom 11:23).

Finally, Paul speaks of the hardening of heart on the part of Israel, which has as its objective the salvation of the Gentiles. "All Israel will be saved" (Rom 11:26) remains unclear to biblical scholars. Does Paul mean that Israel will be saved by God's mercy without any mass conversion of Jews? Is his intention to assert that God will exercise his mercy at the *parousia* (the final coming) and save Israel without faith in Christ, or does the apostle mean that Yahweh will deliver his covenant people without reference to conversion? Whatever be God's plan, "they are beloved for the sake of their ancestors" (Rom 11:28), and it all belongs to the realm of "mystery": "I want you to understand this mystery" (Rom 11:25).

Paul continues his exposition in terms of God, who incorporated into his plan of mercy both Jewish and Gentile failure to obey: "Just as you were once disobedient to God but now have received mercy because of their disobedience, so they have now been disobedient in order that by the mercy shown to you, they also may receive mercy. For God has consigned all people to disobedience, that he may have mercy upon all" (Rom 11:30–32).

Finally, Paul cries out in praise of God's mercy using a hymn that is thought to have derived from the Christian community in the early days of the church.

O the depths of the riches and wisdom and
    knowledge of God!
How unsearchable are his judgments and how
    inscrutable his ways!
For who has known the mind of the Lord,
    or who has been his counselor?
Or who has given a gift to him that he might be repaid.
For from him and through him and to him
    are all things.
To him be glory and praise for ever. Amen.
    (Rom 11:33–36)

For Reflection

1. What does having faith in God mean to you? Are you able to trust that God is serious, that we are made righteous through faith?
2. If we are declared righteous through faith, what role do good works play in our lives?
3. When we consider the stumbling blocks we encounter daily, it is easier for us to understand how it was that Israel allowed Christ be a stumbling block for them. What things are for you a stumbling block in upright living?

Prayer by St. Francis Xavier
Missionary, Patron of the Missions (d. 1552)

ETERNAL GOD, CREATOR OF ALL THINGS,
    Remember that you alone created the souls
        of unbelievers,
        which You have made according to Your Image
           and Likeness....

Remember, O Lord, Your Son Jesus Christ,
    Who so generously shed His Blood and suffered
        for them.
Do not permit that Your Son, Our Lord, remain
    unknown by unbelievers…
With the help of Your Saints and the Church, the
    Bride of Your Son,
    Remember your mercy, forget their idolatry and
        infidelity,
    and make them know Him, Whom You have sent,
Jesus Christ, Your Son, Our Lord,
    Who is our salvation, our life, and our resurrection,
    through Whom we have been saved and
        redeemed,
    and to Whom is due glory forever. Amen.[112]

Summary of the Main Points
in the Letter to the Romans

Paul addresses the Roman Church, one that he did not found, concerning justification and how, through Christ's death on the cross, he took on our debt of sin and its consequences. Both Jews and Gentiles had sinned, and both stood under the hand of God's wrath. But Christ achieved our righteousness that comes to the baptized Christian through faith. A life lived in the Spirit is our pass to salvation as well as our response to God's gift of justification through Christ.

FOR FURTHER READING

Byrne, S.J., Brendan. *Romans.* Sacra Pagina Series. Collegeville, MN: The Liturgical Press, 1996.

Fitzmyer, S.J., Joseph A., "The Letter to the Romans," in *The New Jerome Biblical Commentary.* Raymond E. Brown et al., eds. Englewood Cliffs, NJ: Prentice Hall, 1990, pp. 830–68.

———. *Spiritual Exercises Based on Paul's Epistle to the Romans.* Mahwah, NJ: Paulist Press, 1995.

Heil, John Paul. *Paul's Letter to the Romans. A Reader Response Commentary.* Mahwah, NJ: Paulist Press, 1987.

Letter to the Colossians

⣿⣿⣿⣿⣿⣿⣿⣿⣿⣿⣿⣿⣿⣿⣿⣿⣿⣿⣿⣿⣿⣿⣿⣿⣿⣿⣿⣿⣿

INTRODUCTION

Colossae, located in Phrygia on the southern bank of the Lycus River, had been an important city in Asia Minor a few centuries before the Christian era. Because of its wool industry, it became a commercial city. By the first century A.D., however, two neighboring cities, Laodicea and Hierapolis, had gained greater status. Its population was principally Gentile, comprised of Greeks and Phrygians, and there was a good number of Jews as well as a result of relocation by Antiochus III in the second century B.C.[113]

The authorship of the Letter to the Colossians is uncertain. Recent biblical scholars are of the opinion that it could have been written by one of Paul's co-workers shortly before his death, perhaps by Timothy (mentioned in Col 1:1), while Paul was in prison.[114] Paul, it appears, believes that his life is coming to an end and that he will not be visiting Colossae again. Thus, he urges the church to accept the authority of his co-workers who are sent to them—Epaphras (Col 1:6–8), Tychicus, Onesimus, Aristarchus, Mark, Jesus who is called Justice, Luke, Demas and Archippus (Col 4:7–18).

Other scholars maintain it is a post-Pauline letter because of its commendation of "household codes" as a way of living in this world. Household codes found in Colossians (e.g., Col 3:18–4:1) were a Roman means of assuring order within its domain. There is no reference to them in the earlier, authentic Pauline letters. For the author of Colossians, the household code has been adapted to the Christian life as a way to live responsibly in the Roman Empire while maintaining one's Christian culture and orientation toward one's heavenly home.[115] The opinion of this writer is that the author of Colossians was Paul in his last days who made use of a scribe to pen this letter. If the author of the letter was not Paul himself, he was well schooled in the theology of Paul.

Because the Letter to the Colossians shares many aspects in common with the Letter to the Ephesians, it is likely that the author of Ephesians was familiar with that letter. In both letters, the vocabulary and style, concepts and concerns are distinct from the letters that are generally accepted as genuine Pauline letters. The Christology[116] of Colossians is derived from a hymn (Col 1:15–18) that the author received from earlier church tradition—Christ is "the image of the invisible God" (Col 1:15), "the first-born from the dead" (Col 1:18), "in him all the fullness of God was pleased to dwell" (Col 1:19) and so on.[117]

If the Letter to the Colossians dates from the last years of his life, it probably was written before the destruction by an earthquake of some cities in the Lycus Valley in A.D. 60–61. But if the letter is post-Pauline, then a date between A.D. 70 and 80 is probable and accounts for the advanced Christology and insights about the delayed coming of the Lord. Ephesus may have been the location from which the writer sent his letter because Paul was imprisoned there.

Epaphroditus is possibly the founder of the church in Colossae. Speaking of the gospel having been preached to them, the author of Colossians acknowledges that they "learned it from Epaphras our beloved fellow servant. He is a faithful minister of Christ on our behalf, and has made known to us your love in the Spirit" (Col 1:7–8). According to Acts 19, Paul's missionary activity in Ephesus reached all of Asia with the assistance of his co-workers.

From various remarks in the letter to Colossae, one is led to conclude that the Colossians were Gentiles. For example, the writer refers to their past: "And you who were dead in trespasses and the uncircumcision of your flesh, God made alive" (Col 2:13). Circumcision was peculiar to the Jewish people as a sign of their covenant with God. "Uncircumcision" then most likely referred to the Gentiles.

The letter was written to encourage the Christian community at Colossae to be faithful to the teachings they had learned and not to be given to popular ideas circulating in their environment. The false teaching to which the author refers was a mixture of Christianity, Judaism, astrology, pagan cults and mystery religions. It seems to have been philosophical in that the author warns the church: "See to it that no one makes prey of you by philosophy and empty deceit, according to human tradition, according to elemental spirits of the universe, and not according to Christ" (Col 2:8).

Reference to angels probably indicates that the Colossians were engaging in angel worship, which was so common in Asia Minor at that time. The writer warns them: "Let no one disqualify you, insisting on self-abasement and worship of angels" (Col 2:18). The Colossians were without doubt returning to some of their former beliefs about intermediate angelic beings that controlled the universe and the destiny of human beings. They were given to ascetical practices in attempts to appease these powerful forces (Col 2:20–23). The author of the letter, therefore, seeks to correct the false teaching that anyone other than Christ is intermediary between human beings and God. Even the angels, including the most powerful ones, are subject to him.[118]

Colossians and Ephesians most likely reflect a transition of leadership from Paul to his co-workers, and then to a period in which both have died and church structures begin to operate.[119]

Outline of the Letter to the Colossians

Greetings, Thanksgiving and Prayer (Col 1:1–14)
  I. The Christological Hymn (Col 1:15–23)
  II. Paul's Ministry and Teaching (Col 1:24–4:6)
Final Greeting and Blessing (Col 4:7–18)

I. THE POWER OF LIVING GOD'S WORD

Preparation: Read Colossians 1:1 through 14. Notice the great wonder and gratitude on Paul's part for the faith of the Colossians who live in a culture of idolatry in which angel worship was so prevalent.

> We always thank God, the Father of our Lord Jesus Christ when we pray for you, because we have heard of your faith in Christ Jesus and of the love which you have for all the saints, because of the hope laid up for you in heaven. Of this you have heard before in the word of the truth, the gospel which has come to you, as indeed in the whole world it is bearing fruit and growing—so among yourselves, from the day you heard and understood the grace of God in truth, as you learned it from Epaphras....So, from the day we heard of it, we have not ceased to pray for you, asking that you may be filled with the knowledge of his will in all spiritual wisdom and understanding, to lead a life worthy of the Lord, fully pleasing to him, bearing fruit in every good work and increasing in the knowledge of God....He has delivered us from the dominion of darkness and transferred us to the kingdom of his

beloved Son, in whom we have redemption, the forgiveness of sins. (Col 1:1–14)

Paul gives thanks to God for maintaining the Colossians in
their faith and for having fueled their love of "the saints" (a title
applied to believers in Paul's letters). He does not congratulate
the Colossians for their spiritual progress, but rather notes that
he thanks God whose work it is in them.[120] The Colossians have
not lived their faith passively. They have witnessed to what God
has worked in them. Theirs has been a contemplative life in
action, allowing God to work through them, and, thus, the
gospel is bearing fruit.

Paul speaks of their "faith in Christ Jesus." By faith "in Christ
Jesus," the apostle is referring not to the object of their faith, but
faith as they live it in the sphere of Christ's lordship. This kind of
faith works itself out in "love," that is, in service of others.
"Hope" is the anchor of faith and love. The hope of which Paul
speaks is anchored in the gospel, already present in Christ, but
whose revelation in glory is in the future, that is, yet to come in
its fullness.[121] It is "the hope laid up...in heaven" (Col 1:4).
These three virtues "establish the Colossians' relationship with
God as Father" and "describes their new and intimate union
'with Christ Jesus.' "[122]

The gospel that is bearing fruit in Colossae is repeated and
multiplied throughout the world, Paul tells the Colossians (Col
1:6). One can almost hear the voice of the aging apostle as he
testifies with excitement to the power of the gospel.

Paul assures the Colossians that he continues to pray for
them that they may be filled with the knowledge of God's
will "in all spiritual wisdom and understanding" (Col 1:9).
Perhaps Paul is making reference to the false wisdom offered
the Colossians by those who "may delude [them] with
beguiling speech" (Col 2:4), those "who make a prey of
[them] by philosophy and empty deceit, according to human

tradition…and not according to Christ" (Col 2:8). Paul prays for them that the Spirit might enlighten them and strengthen them "with all power" (Col 1:11) so that they might face trial and opposition with patient endurance, "with joy, giving thanks to the Father" (Col 1:12).

The gift of redemption in Christ, Paul writes to the Colossians, was a deliverance from "the dominion of darkness," and we were "transferred to the kingdom of his beloved Son, in whom we have the forgiveness of sins" (Col 1:14). We were redeemed, forgiven our sins and admitted to the kingdom of the Son of God in our baptism. What greater gift could one imagine? What honor, praise and thanksgiving is due our God!

Today's Christians continue to be beset by false teachers who offer easy solutions to basic mysteries of the faith. Prayer for one another in such circumstances is consonant with Paul's own expression of friendship and support. At such moments in life, the faithful believer must turn to his or her baptismal creed, to the faith that she or he was taught (Col 2:6).

For Reflection

1. What teachings of the church have been challenged in your lifetime?
2. What is an appropriate response to such challenges in view of the Letter to the Colossians?
3. Read and reflect on the creed we use at Sunday Mass. Thank God for each of these gifts of his love that are enumerated in the creed.

Prayer of Saint Elizabeth Ann Seton
First American Saint; d. 1821; Canonized Sept 14, 1975

May the most high,
>the most just
>>and the most holy will of God
>be praised,
>>adored,
>>>and loved. Amen.[123]

II. HYMN TO CHRIST

Preparation: Read Colossians 1:15–23 in which Paul utilizes a hymn of the early church, one of the few resources for theology to which Paul had access.

He is the image of the invisible God,
>the first of all creation;
for in him all things were created,
>in heaven and on the earth,
visible and invisible,
>whether thrones or dominions
>or principalities or authorities—
>all things were created through him and for him.
He is before all things,
>and in him all things hold together.
He is head of the body, the church;
>he is the beginning,
>the first-born from the dead,
>that in everything he might be pre-eminent.
For in him all the fullness of God was pleased to dwell,
>and through him to reconcile to himself all things,

> whether on earth, or in heaven,
> making peace by the blood of his cross.
>   (Col 1:15–20)

The poetic character of this passage is obvious from first reading. Most biblical scholars today believe that it was a very early Christian hymn, which the writer of the letter inserted as a means of instruction for the Colossians. Hymns were used by the early Christians not only to honor the Lord at liturgical services, such as the Lord's Supper and baptism, but also as a catechetical tool to ensure the transmission of the church's beliefs concerning the identity of Jesus.[124] The rhythm and rhyme of hymns made it easy for people to learn and remember them. Thus, the author exhorts his readers to "sing psalms and hymns and spiritual songs with thankfulness in your hearts to God" (Col 3:16). There was not much in the way of theology to draw from in the time of Paul except for hymns such as this.[125]

The hymn in Colossians may be understood from its structure of two stanzas: (1) Colossians 1:15–18, which gives expression to the Son's work in creation. He is the agent of creation, both of the visible and the invisible world, and the means of its cohesion. (2) Colossians 1:19–20, which indicates Christ's renewal of all created things through his death and resurrection. He is head of the church as well as its Lord and redeemer.

This hymn is one of the richest sources for theological insights about the identity of Jesus Christ. It reflects elements from wisdom literature of the Old Testament (for example, The Book of Wisdom, Proverbs, etc.), which was very popular in the first century.

Soon after the death and resurrection of Jesus, when the early Christians began to understand who Jesus was, they applied wisdom themes to their risen Lord. "He is the image of the invisible God" (Col 1:15). In other words, Jesus Christ reveals to us who God is in his very person. "Image" *(eikon)* in Greek indicates more than a representation; it conveys the essence, the very nature, of that represented.[126] Jesus is not just a copy of God; he is the perfect revelation of the invisible God. "Image" communicates the idea that Christ makes visible the God who is invisible.

"He is the first-born of all creation" (Col 1:15b). Here the hymn draws on Proverbs, which many scholars see as a foreshadowing of the trinity that was revealed by Jesus in his incarnation:

> The LORD begot me, the first-born of his ways,
>   the forerunner of his prodigies of long ago;
> From of old I was poured forth,
>   at the first, before the earth....
> When he established the heavens I was there....
> Then was I beside him as his craftsman,
>   and I was his delight day by day. (Prov 8:22–30; NAB)

Like wisdom personified, Christ is pre-existent with God through whom creation came to be and by whom all created beings are held in unity (Col 1:15–17). As the "first-born," Jesus Christ stands beyond the created world; he is the very agent by which everything came into being. Thus as "first-born of all creation," he is related to creation as its first-born. He is also the "first-born" of "a new community of believers that is to be glorified."[127] In the second century, the Arians misinterpreted this phrase as proof of the heresy they taught—Jesus was a created being. "He is before all things" (Col 1:17) was used by Arius in the late third century to argue that Christ had a beginning and therefore was not God but human.

"He is head of the body, the church" (Col 1:18). Among the Greeks, there was the belief that the cosmos was filled by a deity. The deity was its head and the rest of the cosmos was its body. In its pastoral approach, the early church was able to use an idea with which the Greeks were familiar and build on the structural notion. Therefore, Christ is the head; he is the divine logos ("Word") and the body is not the cosmos, but rather the church.

"He is the beginning, the first-born from among the dead" (Col 1:18b). Jesus was the first human (though still divine) to rise from the dead. This signals that others, all faithful Christians, will follow him in rising from the dead. In that sense, Jesus Christ was the first-born of all of us who are yet to rise from the dead.

As the second stanza of the hymn denotes, Jesus is more than a mere human. "God was pleased to have all his fullness dwell in him" (Col 1:19); that is, the full nature of God dwells in Jesus Christ; exclusively in him does God dwell in all fullness.

God, by becoming human in the person of Jesus, recreated fallen creation by reconciling "to himself all things, whether on earth or in heaven, making peace by the blood of his cross" (Col 1:20). God's love in Jesus has no limits; it includes the whole of the cosmos. "All things" were brought into harmony through his blood on the cross.

The hymn gives us a mixture of both human and divine Christology. It is this "mixture" that was a scandal to the Jews. How could the God they worshiped be present in Jesus who accepted death on a cross? Every Jew knew that one who was hanged as a criminal on the cross was cursed by God: "If a man guilty of a capital offense is put to death and his corpse hung on a tree, it shall not remain on the tree overnight. You shall bury it the same day; otherwise, since God's curse rests on him who hangs on a tree, you will defile the land" (Deut 21:22–23; NAB).

One might say that the scandal of the cross remains alive today. The humility and obedience that Jesus exhibited through his passion and death are not virtues that are valued by the world today. If the body of Christ, the church, is humble and obedient as is Christ the head, it too is a stumbling block.

For Reflection

1. This hymn puts us in touch with the spirit of the early church. What, if anything, does that do for your faith?

2. What does it mean to you that you are part of that body, the church, of which Christ himself is the head?

3. Is the Letter to the Colossians significant today? Does the use of fortune tellers or Ouija boards, for example, indicate a false understanding of Christ's role?

PRAYER: O Wisdom
(The First of the Greater Antiphons of Vespers, the Western Rite)

O WISDOM,
> who camest out of the mouth of the Most High,
> and reachest from one end to another,
> mightily and sweetly ordering all things:
COME and teach us the way of prudence.[128]

III. LIFE IN THE LORD

Preparation: Read Colossians 1:24 through 4:18 wherein Paul discusses his role as apostle, attacks the teachings of the false teachers and sets forth guidelines for living in Christ.

> As…you received Christ Jesus the Lord, so live in him, rooted and built up in him and established in the faith, just as you were taught, abounding in thanksgiving.…For in him the whole fullness of deity dwells bodily, and you have come to fullness of life in him, who is the head of all rule and authority. In him you were circumcised with a circumcision made without hands, by putting off the body of flesh in the circumcision of Christ; and you were buried with him in baptism, in which you were also raised with him through faith in the working of God, who raised him from the dead. And you…God made alive

together with him, having forgiven us all our trespasses, having canceled the bond which stood against
us with its legal demands; this he set aside, nailing it to
the cross. He disarmed principalities and powers and
made a public example of them, triumphing over
them in him. (Col 2:6–15)

In this section we have the major teachings about Christ,
which are set forth as a corrective of the false teaching that has
crept into the church at Colossae by some adversaries of the faith.
In the first two verses, Colossians 2:6–7, the church members are
exhorted "to live in him" (Col 2:6), that is, to live that tradition of
"Christ Jesus the Lord" that they received. By that tradition, they
have been "rooted" (in Greek, *errizomenoi*)[129] or firmly fixed in
Christ at baptism. The root, which gets life from the Lord Jesus,
corresponds to the baptized person. Hence, the Colossians receive
directly from Christ his own life by which they now live. They are
also "built up in him" and "established in the faith" by the teaching or tradition handed on to them. For these tremendous gifts,
the proper Christian response is gratitude.

Because of the fact that "in him [Christ] the whole fullness of
deity dwells bodily" (Col 2:9), the Christian, rooted and built up
in him, also shares the fullness of the life of God. The false teaching that the adversaries offer cannot compare with this great
mystery won by Christ for us. Christ is not just another spiritual
force among others that were presented to the Colossians by
false teachers. Rather, Christ is "the head of all rule and authority" (Col 2:10). Therefore, they need not look for any other
beings to supplement Christ because he is the fullness of God.

Obviously the false teachers have added a Jewish flavor to
their rainbow of teachings. The writer of Colossians, however,
assures the Gentile church that circumcision of the flesh, which
put the Jew in relationship with God as one of his people, is not
necessary. They were accepted into relationship with Christ

whose very life they constantly share. They were "buried with him in baptism" (Col 2:12); this imagery of burial derives from the baptismal immersion, and rising with him "in faith" comes from emergence afterward. This symbolism dramatizes the renunciation of the life of sin and the beginning of a new life in Christ. Not only were they forgiven their sins (Col 2:13), but God also, through the cross, "canceled the bond which stood against us with its legal demands" (Col 2:14); that is, the debt incurred by our sins has been canceled and replaced by our union with Christ.

The disarmament of the "principalities and powers" (Col 2:15) utilizes the image of a triumphant general who returned from battle and entered the imperial city leading his captives, thus making of them a "public example." Christ has triumphed over his enemies, and the baptized person shares in his victory; no longer are they captives of their former lives.

For Reflection

1. Because all the members of the church form one body with Christ as its head, what does sin do to the church?
2. What does being "rooted" in Christ mean to you?
3. Are there people in the church today similar to the adversaries at work in the church at Colossae?

Prayer to Do Always the Will of God
St. Teresa of Avila: Doctor of the Church (d. 1584)

O LORD,
  regulate all things by your wisdom,
    so that I may always serve you in the manner that
    you will.
  Do not punish me by granting what I will

if it offends against your love,
for I want your love to live always in me.
Help me to deny myself in order that I may serve you.
Let me live for you—who in yourself are the true
life. Amen.[130]

**Summary of the Main Points in the
Letter to the Colossians**

The Letter to the Colossians was probably penned by a
scribe of the apostle either shortly before Paul's death or
after. It addresses a period in which the faithful were
adjusting to the absence or death of their hero and leader,
St. Paul. In addition, false teachers had made inroads into
the thinking and faith expression of the Colossians. Paul
reminds the Colossians of traditional teachings that counteract the untruths that won the thinking of some of the
people in the Colossian Church. The letter helps to
bridge the period of transition of authority from Paul and
his co-workers to later church structures.

FOR FURTHER READING

"Colossians." *The Catholic Study Bible*. Oxford: Oxford University Press, 1990, Reading Guide, pp. 518–22.

Horgan, Maurya P., "The Letter to the Colossians," in *The New
Jerome Biblical Commentary*. Raymond E. Brown et al, eds.
Englewood Cliffs, NJ: Prentice Hall, 1990, pp. 876–82.

MacDonald, Margaret Y. *Colossians and Ephesians*. Sacra Pagina
Series. Collegeville, MN: The Liturgical Press, 2000.

Thurston, Bonnie. *Reading Colossians, Ephesians and 2 Thessalonians. A Literary and Theological Commentary.* New York: Crossroad Publishing Co., 1995.

Letter to the Ephesians

INTRODUCTION

There is considerable disagreement as to whether the Letter to the Ephesians was actually written by Paul. Fr. Raymond E. Brown maintains that today about 80 percent of scholars commenting on this letter believe that it was not a letter from the apostle.[131] Although this topic is given much attention in most commentaries, it does not add much to the purpose of this writing to enter into the discussion except simply to note a few differences between the Letter to the Ephesians and the undisputed letters of Paul.

1. Some indications in the letter point to a church that has never been founded nor taught by Paul personally: "…because I have heard of your faith" (Eph 1:15).
2. The vocabulary and style of writing are distinct from other letters that are indisputably of Pauline origin.
3. The concept of the universal church in Ephesians replaces Paul's concern for the local church, along with its triumphs and difficulties, as found in the letters he wrote.
4. The notion of the church being "built upon the foundation of the apostles and prophets" (Eph 2:20) seems to reflect a

later period in the church, as does the presumption of a church in which Jews and Gentiles are already integrated.[132]

In my opinion, the evidence within the Letter to the Ephesians points to a later period of development in the church than that presented in Paul's own letters. It has a much more general tone also than Paul's letters, and its contents are of such nature that it could be sent to more than one church community.[133] The emphasis regarding eschatology[134] in the Ephesians letter is more focused on the future of Christ's coming, whereas in the authentic Pauline writings, the focus is more on an imminent return of the Lord in glory.

Nevertheless, the author of this Deutero-Pauline[135] letter is well versed in Pauline theology and probably belonged to a church community founded by Paul, which passed on his teachings to a later generation. The Letter to the Ephesians was likely written in the late first century, between the years 80 and 100. Use of another person's name in writing a letter was not uncommon at that time. It was a practice in which a "school of theology" transmitted the valuable teachings of a renowned person to a new age in the church and was understood in that sense by the addressees.

For whom was the letter intended? The greeting of the letter does not include the location of the church, as "at Ephesus," as do Paul's letters to other churches. In some ancient but later and less reliable manuscripts, there is found "who are at Ephesus" in the greeting, which may indicate its first use in Ephesus or that Ephesus was the most important of several other church locations. For that reason, much of scholarly opinion suggests that this letter was intended for several churches in Asia. As Fr. Raymond Brown aptly states: "Especially appealing to an ecumenical age is the magnificent Ephesian view of the church universal and of unity among Christians."[136]

Outline of the Letter to the Ephesians

Opening and Thanksgiving (Eph 1:1–23)
  I. Pauline Instructions (Eph 2:1–3:21)
  II. Pauline Exhortations (Eph 4:1–6:20)
Conclusion: Mission and Blessings (Eph 6:21–24)

I. CITIZENS WITH THE SAINTS

Preparation: Read Ephesians 1:1 through 3:21 in which the author greets the church and blesses God who has redeemed both Jew and Gentile and reconciled them to one another in Christ, thus making them a new humanity.

> So then you are no longer strangers and sojourners, but you are fellow citizens with the saints and members of the household of God built upon the foundation of the apostles and prophets, Christ Jesus himself being the cornerstone, in whom the whole structure is joined together and grows into a holy temple in the Lord; in whom you also are built into it for a dwelling place of God in the Spirit. (Eph 2:19–22)

This passage takes up and summarizes the previous verses regarding the situation of the Gentiles before baptism. They were considered "aliens" in relation to Israel. Reminding them of their past, the author of Ephesians exhorts his readers to "remember that you were at that time separated from Christ, alienated from the commonwealth of Israel, and strangers to the covenants of promise, having no hope and without God in the world" (Eph 2:12). But now they "are no longer strangers and sojourners" (Eph 2:19a). Now they are one with the Jews, a union brought about "in the blood of Christ" (Eph 2:13b). By baptism they became people of God on equal footing as Israel, as the prophet Isaiah foretold of the two groups: "I, the Creator, who gave them life. Peace, peace to the far and the near, says the Lord, and I will heal them" (Isa 57:19). The writer wants his Gentile readers to understand and appreciate what God has done on their behalf by reconciling them with the Jews and by bringing them into the household of God: "You are fellow citizens with the saints and members of the household of God" (Eph 2:19b). They now belong to the same ecclesial (that is, church) family as the writer noted earlier in the letter: "He destined us in love to be his sons through Jesus Christ, according to the purpose of his will" (Eph 1:5).

Their present situation of unity was certainly progress for the Gentile and Jewish Christians when compared to the situation at the time of Paul. The struggles over differences regarding observance of the law were wedges of division between them.

Their present status is the result of Christ's gift of love on the cross, which made the Jews and the Gentiles "one new person," *hena kainon anthropon* (Eph 2:15). The use of the Greek word *kainos* for "new" instead of *neos* (new in the sense of new among others of the same quality) is significant. *Kainos* ("new") indicates a creation of something that is of different quality.

Through Christ's death and resurrection, God reconciled the Jews and Gentiles so that both of them have become "members of the household of God" (Eph 2:19b), a status that was never possible before baptism. Both Jew and Gentile now share the position of "beloved children" of God (Eph 5:1). Households in the first century consisted of parents, children and slaves. The baptized are not as slaves in God's household; they are God's own children who have inherited "the riches of his glorious inheritance" (Eph 1:18b).

The church is "built upon the foundation of the apostles and prophets" (Eph 2:20). The writer now turns to the image of a building. The Gentiles, because of the reconciliation brought about by Christ, are no longer without family or common-wealth. They have been "raised up with him [Christ]," and made to "sit with him in the heavenly places in Christ Jesus" (Eph 2:6). As such, the Jewish and Gentile Christians have been built up into a structure, a building, "Christ Jesus himself being the cornerstone" (Eph 2:20).

This structure, the church, is composed of bricks joined securely together, and in that structure God is present.

> Like a well-constructed building, the Church united the two Christianities of the Jews and the Gentiles. From Judaism, God fashioned noble foundation stones, squared, polished and precious. They were the holy remnant....Under Paul's eyes, when the first quarry had been worked out, the Gentiles provided the materials needed to go on with the building.[137]

The cornerstone, which is Christ himself, holds the whole thing together so that all the parts are fitted together in Christ. The foundation is made up by the apostles and prophets (that is, "prophets" of the early church); the stones of the building are all of the baptized; the cornerstone is Christ. There is no room for divisions; God has created a new entity in which unity is provided by the structure. The Jerusalem Temple is replaced by a divine-human church with Christ as its head and the faithful as its members; the church is now the focus of God's presence.

Thus the author seeks to bring together a church threatened from outside by enemies of Christ and the church and from inside by apparent divisions between Jewish Christians and Gentile Christians.

For Reflection

1. Why is unity in the church important?
2. What are the difficulties today that inhibit the unity of the church?
3. If each church member would see himself or herself as one of the metaphorical bricks, what do you think would happen in the church?

Prayer from the Common of the Dedication of a Church

> God Our Father,
> from living stones, your chosen people,
> you built an eternal temple to your glory.
> Increase the spiritual gifts you have given to your Church
> that your faithful people may continue to grow
> into the new and eternal Jerusalem.
> We ask this through our Lord Jesus Christ, your Son,
> who lives and reigns with you and the holy Spirit,
> one God, for ever and ever. Amen.[138]

II. CHRIST, THE HEAD OF THE CHURCH

Preparation: Read Ephesians 4:1 through 6:24. The author, after speaking of a new humanity created by God out of a divided humanity, points out the incongruity of the conduct of unconverted Gentiles with the oneness that the body of Christ implies.

> Be subject to one another out of reverence for Christ.
> Wives, be subject to your husbands, as to the Lord. For
> the husband is the head of the wife as Christ is the
> head of the church, his body, and is himself its Savior.

As the church is subject to Christ, so let wives also be subject in everything to their husbands. Husbands, love your wives, as Christ loved the church and gave himself up for her, that he might sanctify her, having cleansed her by the washing of water with the word, that he might present the church to himself in splendor, without spot or wrinkle or any such thing, that she might be holy and without blemish. Even so husbands should love their wives as their own bodies. He who loves his wife loves himself. For no man ever hates his own flesh, but nourishes and cherishes it, as Christ does the church, because we are members of his body. "For this reason a man shall leave his father and mother and be joined to his wife, and the two shall become one flesh." This mystery is a profound one, and I am saying that it refers to Christ and the church; however, let each one of you love his wife as himself, and let the wife see that she respects her husband. (Eph 5:22–33)

Two themes come together in this passage—the love between husband and wife, and the love between Christ and his church. They are both at the service of one another. In the household codes, the wife was subordinate to her husband. Thus, to demonstrate that the church is subject to Christ and owes him obedience and love, the imagery of husband and wife is used. The husband is to have a deep, selfless love *(agape)* for his wife, even as Christ loved the church to the point of giving his life for her.[139]

This passage, which "attests to a high spiritual estimation of marriage,"[140] upholds its sacredness and nobility. Nevertheless, in the last decades, Eph 5:22–32 has been the focus of much controversy among both men and women. The question has been asked, "Should it be eradicated from the church's lectionary of readings for Mass?" Still others have insisted that it should be excised from the New Testament itself on the basis of its use by some men to justify oppressive action against women.

Certainly, to come to conclusions that support domination of women would be contrary to the teachings of Jesus and to the church as well. The problem lies in the extraction of some isolated parts from the context of the letter as a whole, a practice that necessarily results in faulty interpretation of the text.

There are aspects within the letter as a whole that demonstrate that an oppressive interpretation was not intended by the author. Early in the letter, the writer maintains that God "chose us in him [Christ] before the foundation of the world, that we should be holy and blameless before him" (Eph 1:4). He goes on to say that in God's plan before the creation of the world, he destined us to be children of God. This adoption would be made possible through the death and resurrection of Jesus Christ (Eph 1:5). It makes no sense then to maintain that oppression or domination would fit into God's eternal plan of making us offspring, nor that sin would be included in God's plan. God's plan was to unite all things in Christ, "things in heaven and things on earth" (Eph 1:10).

Again, it is highly unlikely, for example, that God would unite a sinful people, engaged in oppression, with his sinless Son and mother. That no one is called by God to be a slave is demonstrated by sacred history in God's deliverance of the Israelites from slavery in Egypt. Moreover, the Ephesians were admonished to "be kind to one another, tenderhearted, forgiving one another, as God in Christ forgave you" (Eph 4:32). "Therefore be imitators of God, as beloved children" (Eph 5:1). They were not to participate "in the unfruitful works of darkness" (Eph 5:11).

The household codes (i.e., the order of subordination of members of a household) that were operative in the Graeco-Roman world are reflected in this passage. A structure of subjection (i.e., wife to husband; children to their fathers; slaves to their masters) was the rule of governance that ensured order in the home and subsequently in the empire. It is possible that Christianity adopted these codes to counteract accusations from outside the church that Christians undermined the order of the state. (A similar code is found in Col 3:18–4:1.) The code of conduct in the Letter to the Ephesians most likely had as its major purpose the establishment of behavior that would distinguish the Christian household from non-Christian ones.[141]

Love for one another, in imitation of Christ who loved us unto his death, is one aspect that defines a Christian. Therefore, the Ephesians are exhorted to "be subject to one another out of reverence for Christ" (Eph 5:21). The "subjection" applies to husbands in relation to their wives as well as wives to their husbands.[142] This mutual subjection stood in stark contrast to that of the social conventions of that time in which women had no rights.

This focus of attention then has to be Christ's relationship with the church. That is the key to understanding the passage. One must ask then, "How did Christ love the church?" He gave his life out of love for it. That is the quality of love required of the husband for his wife, a love that is totally unselfish and totally self-giving.

In Ephesians 5:26–27, Jesus is presented as the bridegroom of the church. The Gentile converts were most certainly aware of the ancient Near Eastern marriage of the gods. Against that background, the author states that Christ washes her (i.e., his bride, the church) clean by the waters of baptism with the word of God that accompanies it. Once cleansed, the church is "clothed in her dowry of holiness and purity"[143] "that he might present the church to himself in splendor...that she might be holy and without blemish" (Eph 5:27). Here we see clearly the theology of the apostle Paul, who wrote of the local church at Corinth: "I feel a divine jealousy for you, for I betrothed you to Christ to present you as a pure bride to her one husband"

(2 Cor 11:2). In Ephesians, the notion of Christ as the bride of the church is applied to the universal church.

The observation that "husbands should love their wives as their own bodies," and that "no man ever hates his own flesh, but nourishes and cherishes it, as Christ does the church" (Eph 5:28–30) elevates marriage to a high level. It is also a reminder of the close relationship of Christ to his church. He nourishes her with the gift of himself—his body and blood in the Eucharist. That is the reason, says the writer, that a man leaves his parents and becomes one flesh with his wife (Eph 5:31).

The whole passage is summed up in Ephesians 5:33: mutual love and respect are modeled by Christ in his love for the church, a love that is symbolized by the church as the bride of Christ. Just so, similar mutuality in love and respect is required in a Christian marriage. Mutual love would require that husband and wife be subordinate to one another and, in imitation of Christ, that both be self-sacrificing in their relationship.

For Reflection

1. The image of the church as the bride of Christ is the model for Christian marriage. In what ways did Christ show his love for the church?
2. How would you explain this passage to another person who holds that this letter is responsible for domestic abuse?
3. What advice would you offer a young couple who asks, "How can we make our marriage last 'until death do us part'?"

Prayer for a Fiancée or Wife
Temple Gairdner (d. A.D. 1928)

That I may come near to her,
    draw me nearer to thee than to her;
    that I may know her,
    make me to know thee more than her;
    that I may love her with the perfect love
      of a perfectly whole heart.
Cause me to love thee more than her and most of all.
    Amen. Amen.
That nothing may be between me and her,
    be thou between us, every moment.
That we may be constantly together,
    draw us into separate loneliness with thyself.
And when we meet breast to breast, my God,
    let it be on thine own. Amen. Amen.[144]

Summary of the Main Points in the Letter to the Ephesians

Given the impersonal tone of the Letter to the Ephesians plus its use of *ekklesia* ("church") for the universal church rather than the local church, it was probably written to be read in several churches rather than to one single church. There is a strong intent in the letter, it seems, to mend divisions between Jews and Gentiles in the church. Baptism has rendered them children of God and "members of the household of God." Therefore, it is fitting that Christian love be self-giving in imitation of Christ. The church is described as the bride of Christ for whom he gave his life.

FOR FURTHER READING

Johnson, Luke T. *The Writings of the New Testament*. Philadelphia, PA: Fortress, 1986.

Kobelski, Paul J., "The Letter to the Ephesians," in *The New Jerome Biblical Commentary*. Raymond E. Brown et al, eds. Englewood Cliffs, NJ: Prentice Hall, 1990, pp. 883–90.

MacDonald, Margaret Y. *Colossians and Ephesians*. Sacra Pagina Series. Ed. Daniel J. Harrington, S.J., Collegeville, MN: The Liturgical Press, 2000.

Perkins, Pheme. *Ephesians*. Abingdon New Testament Commentaries. Nashville: Abingdon Press, 1997.

Second Letter
to the Thessalonians

∞∞∞

INTRODUCTION

Did the apostle Paul also write this Letter to the Thessalonians? Whether he wrote the letter or someone from a Pauline school of thought wrote it remains a mystery. Scholarly opinion today leans toward a pseudonymous writer for the Second Letter to the Thessalonians. These biblical scholars point to similarities between the first and second letters, which they consider an indication of a later author using the first letter as a model.[145] The date of writing also enters into the discussion. A time after the death of Paul, which occurred in the 60s, would seem to fit the picture of a persecution, perhaps under Nero who died in A.D. 68 at his own hand. The writing could have been before Nero's death and after the death of Paul, if the writing is indeed pseudonymous.[146]

At the time that the Second Letter to the Thessalonians was written, the Christians were staunch in their faith in the midst of adversity; as the writer affirms: "[Y]our faith is growing abundantly, and the love of every one of you for one another is increasing. Therefore we ourselves boast of you in the churches of God for your steadfastness and faith in all your persecutions and in the afflictions which you are enduring" (2 Thess 1:3–4). Moreover, the Thessalonians' response to suffering has been an example to the other churches in Macedonia and Achia.

The main concern of the author, whom I will refer to as Paul, is that some members of the community are overly preoccupied with the coming of the Lord and maintain that it is imminent. As a result, they refuse to work and live off the rest of the community. The letter seeks to correct this misunderstanding by telling the Thessalonians about certain events that must come to pass before the final coming of the Lord.

Outline of 2 Thessalonians

Opening and Thanksgiving (2 Thess 1:1–12)
I. The Second Coming (2 Thess 2:1–17)
II. Exhortations to Maintain Proper Conduct (2 Thess 3:1–15)
Greetings and Final Blessing (2 Thess 3:17–18)

I. God's Just Judgment

Preparation: Read 2 Thessalonians 1:1 through 1:12. After greeting the Thessalonians, the writer affirms their faith and perseverance in suffering. Those who are responsible for the oppression will be subjected to the wrath of God.

> [W]e ourselves boast of you in the churches of God for your steadfastness and faith in all your persecutions and in the afflictions which you are enduring. This is evidence of the righteous judgment of God, that you may be made worthy of the kingdom of God, for which you are suffering—since indeed

God deems it just to repay with affliction those who afflict you, and to grant rest with us to you who are afflicted, when the Lord Jesus is revealed from heaven with his mighty angels in flaming fire, inflicting vengeance upon those who do not know God and upon those who do not obey the gospel of our Lord Jesus. They shall suffer the punishment of eternal destruction and exclusion from the presence of the Lord and from the glory of his might, when he comes on that day to be glorified in his saints, and to be marveled at in all who have believed, because our testimony to you was believed. To this end we always pray for you, that our God may make you worthy of his call and may fulfill every good resolve and work of faith by his power, so that the name of our Lord Jesus may be glorified in you, and you in him, according to the grace of our God and the Lord Jesus Christ. (2 Thess 1:4–12)

Paul encourages the Thessalonians first in their faith and love for one another, and then in their steadfastness in suffering by which they are being "made worthy of the kingdom of God" (2 Thess 1:5). When the Lord comes, they will be judged as faithful even under affliction, and they will be ready to enjoy admittance into the kingdom of God. The author makes the point that God will reward their perseverance in their trials and sufferings. Likewise, God's divine justice will prevail in punishment for those who inflict adversity upon the faithful.[147] The prophet Isaiah speaks of the justice of God in similar terms:

> I in turn will choose ruthless treatment for them
>   and bring upon them what they fear.
>
> Because, when I called, no one answered,
>   when I spoke, no one listened;

> Because they did what was evil in my sight,
>   and chose what gave me displeasure....
> Lo, the LORD shall come in fire,
>   his chariots like the whirlwind. (Isa 66:4; 15; NAB)

It is God's place alone to inflict vengeance on the evildoer (2 Thess 1:6–7). In Romans 12:17–21, Paul urges the Christians to return good for evil and not seek vengeance themselves. When the judgment comes, those who are afflicted will receive rest in place of their sufferings.

The writer describes the judgment in apocalyptic terms and imagery. Apocalyptic is a religious literature foreign to modern thinking because it is highly symbolic and not to be understood literally. Such writing generally appeared in times of persecution to encourage the faithful. In this passage, we have an example of apocalyptic writing. The Lord is coming from heaven "with his mighty angels in flaming fire" (2 Thess 1:7). The prophet Zechariah spoke of the angels accompanying God at the judgment: "Then the LORD, my God, shall come, and all his holy ones with him" (Zech 14:5). The Gospel of Matthew presents the coming of the Lord in similar terms: He will come "in his glory, and all the angels with him" (Matt 25:31).

Paul says they will come "in flaming fire" (2 Thess 1:7). Fire is frequently used in connection with God's judgment. Fire is an apocalyptic image in scripture that accompanies the public manifestation of God in great force.[148] In Isaiah, God's judgment takes place thus: "Lo, the LORD shall come in fire,/.../To wreak his wrath with burning heat/ and his punishment with fiery flames./ For the LORD shall judge all mankind/by fire and sword" (Isa 66:15–16; NAB).

The people who through their own culpable ignorance do not know God and those who have refused to hear the gospel will suffer "the punishment of eternal destruction and exclusion from the presence of the Lord and from the glory of his might"

(2 Thess 1:9). For Paul, nothing could be worse than separation from God, for his longing was to be with Christ (Phil 1:23).

As for the faithful who have believed the gospel that Paul preached to them, they will participate in the glory of the risen Lord whose glory is to be celebrated in his final coming (2 Thess 1:10). The writer assures the Thessalonians of his prayers for them that they may "be worthy of his call, and may fulfill every good resolve and work of faith by his power" (2 Thess 1:11). They have been called by God at their baptism to be God's people and, finally, to enjoy the blessings of the kingdom (1 Thess 1:4). At the time of this letter, their faith is still the cause of much suffering, so prayers on the part of the one who brought them the gospel and subsequently nourishes their faith with letters are of great worth.

The purpose of Paul's work with the Thessalonians was "that the name of our Lord Jesus" would be glorified in them (2 Thess 1:12). Certainly, for Christ, the glorification of the Christian is likewise glory for him, for he gave his life for that purpose alone.

Many readers today are not attracted to the apocalyptic images the author uses in this letter to speak about the final coming of the Lord. Modern sensibilities often prefer not to deal with that which is not consoling for the individual. Perhaps, though, it is good for us to dwell at times on God's justice as tempered not only with mercy but also in the sense that it gives us what we have freely chosen by our actions during life.

For Reflection

1. The final coming of the Lord, which includes judgment of all people, does not receive much attention today. Yet, each time we pray the creed, we pray "from thence he shall come to judge the living and the dead." Why has this teaching become so obscure?

2. The *Catechism of the Catholic Church* states that the message of the Last Judgment calls all people "to conversion while God is still giving them 'the acceptable time,...the day of salvation.' It inspires a holy fear of God and commits them to the justice of the Kingdom of God" (#1041). Comment on this statement.

3. What does it mean to you that Jesus will come "to be glorified in his saints, and to be marveled at in all who have believed" (2 Thess 1:10)?

Prayer: Lead Kindly Light
John Henry Newman: Convert, Religious Thinker, Cardinal
(d. A.D. 1890)

Lead, kindly Light, amid the encircling gloom, lead Thou
    me on!
The night is dark, and I am far from home—
    Lead Thou me on!
Keep thou my feet; I do not ask to see
    the distant scene—one step enough for me.
I was not ever thus, nor pray'd that Thou
    shouldst lead me on.
I loved to choose and see my path, but no
    Lead Thou me on!
I loved the garish day, and, spite of fears,
Pride ruled my will: remember not past years.
So long Thy power hath blest me, sure it still
    Will lead me on,
O'er moon and fen, o'er crag and torrent, till
    The night is gone;
And with the morn those angel faces smile
which I have loved long since, and lost awhile.[149]

II. Concerning the Day of the Lord

Preparation: Read 2 Thessalonians 2:1 through 2:17 in which the author exhorts the Thessalonians not to be anxious concerning the final coming of the Lord. There are signs that are not yet evident. No one should use the coming of the Lord as an excuse not to work.

> Now concerning the coming of our Lord Jesus Christ and our assembling to meet him, we beg you...not to be quickly shaken in mind or excited, either by spirit or by word, or by letter purporting to be from us, to the effect that the day of the Lord has come. Let no one deceive you in any way; for that day will not come, unless the rebellion comes first, and the man of lawlessness is revealed, the son of perdition, who opposes and exalts himself against every so-called god or object of worship, so that he takes his seat in the temple of God, proclaiming himself to be God. Do you not remember that when I was still with you I told you this? And you know what is restraining him now so that he may be revealed in his time. For the mystery of lawlessness is already at work; only he who now restrains it will do so until he is out of the way. And then the lawless one will be revealed, and the Lord Jesus will slay him with the breath of his mouth and destroy him by his appearing and his coming. The coming of the lawless one by the activity of Satan will be with all power and with pretended signs and wonders, and with all wicked deception for those who are to perish, because they refused to love the truth and so be saved. Therefore God sends upon them a strong delusion, to make them believe what is false, so that all

may be condemned who did not believe the truth but
had pleasure in unrighteousness. (2 Thess 2:1–12)

The uncertainty of the date of the Second Letter to the Thessalonians makes the task of determining the meaning of this passage a difficult one. The central doctrinal issue in the letter is the
Day of the Lord, which is treated in this passage. The author
clearly disapproves of a clock-and-calendar calculation concerning the Lord's return. He also wishes to quell the notion that the
parousia (the coming of the Lord in glory) has already occurred.

There are signs and prerequisite conditions, Paul maintains,
for the Lord's coming in triumph. The writer speaks of "our
assembling to meet him" (2 Thess 2:1). The "assembling" probably refers to the expectation of the Jews that their people, scat-
tered throughout the empire as a result of relocation in times of
persecution and war, would one day be gathered together in
their homeland. Jeremiah, in 2 Maccabees, tells the people: "The
place [where the ark, the tent and the altar were hidden] is to
remain unknown until God gathers his people together again
and shows them mercy" (2 Macc 2:7). The early church applied
this gathering of God's people to the final gathering at the coming of the Lord at the end-time.[150]

The writer wishes to counteract any deception that the Lord
has already come, whether it be by "spirit," "word" or "letter" (2
Thess 2:2), that is, by any means of communication that seeks to
undermine the previous teaching by St. Paul that we cannot cal-
culate the time of his coming.

Before "that day" comes "the rebellion," "and the man of
lawlessness is revealed, the son of perdition" (2 Thess 2:3).
Assuming that the writer is speaking of God as the one
"restraining him now" (2 Thess 2:6) until the gospel is brought
to all peoples, "the man of lawlessness" and "the son of perdition" are probably references to Caligula, the Roman emperor
from A.D. 37 to 41, or Nero (A.D. 54 to 68), or Domitian (A.D.

81 to 96) or even a symbolic figure of the most evil ruler of Jewish history.[151] Antiochus Epiphanes IV (175 to 163 B.C.) became the paradigm for evil to the Jewish people. He defiled the Holy of Holies in the temple by setting up a statue of Zeus and offering sacrifice on the altar.

It is difficult to know to what evil person the author is referring. Emperor Caligula ordered his image to be placed in the Jerusalem temple and proclaimed "himself to be God" (2 Thess 2:4). Nero, much like Antiochus Epiphanes IV, also became a paradigm of evil that must reach its zenith before the Lord's coming. Any one of the three emperors is one whom the Thessalonian readers would remember as usurping that which belonged to God alone.[152] As the embodiment of Satan and his power, "the lawless one" leads a rebellion against God, all the while proclaiming himself to be God. In apocalyptic thinking, God's judgment will come when evil has expended its power.[153]

"For the mystery of lawlessness is already at work" (2 Thess 2:7)—Satan is the "mystery of lawlessness" whose work in the world serves as a counterpart to the mystery of God's purpose. Satan will metaphorically be unmasked at the end-time and shown to be the lie that he is. That is the time that God destroys Satan completely by "the breath of his mouth" (2 Thess 2:8).

The clause "for those who are to perish because they refused to love the truth and so be saved" (2 Thess 2:10) refers to those who have, by their own will, closed their minds to the gospel. To these, God sends a "delusion to make them believe what is false" (2 Thess 2:11). With these words, the author is affirming that God is in control of everything.

Thus the writer accepts that the work of Satan, which precedes the coming of the Lord, is indeed in process. As the writer indicates, however, the coming has not yet occurred, and idleness, as he warns in 2 Thessalonians 3:6–13, is not the proper way to await the coming of the Lord.

For Reflection

1. Jesus told his disciples: "Of that day or that hour no one knows, not even the angels in heaven, nor the Son, but only the Father" (Mark 13:32). What opinions do you hear most often today regarding the coming of the Lord?
2. The *Catechism of the Catholic Church* states that "this consummation will be the final realization of the unity of the human race, which God willed from creation" (#1045). What are you doing as a Christian to assist that unity in the here and now?

Prayer for a Strong Virtue of Hope
St. Mary Magdalene de Pazzi (d. A.D. 1607)

LORD,
    Give me a strong hope, for I cannot attain salvation
        without that virtue being deeply rooted in me.
    This hope is necessary so that I may ask you to pardon
        my sins
        and reach my supernatural end.
    How greatly this hope gladdens me,
        making me firmly expect
            that I will reach heaven, my homeland.
    Even in this life it gives me a foretaste of
        relishing, understanding, and possessing you, my
            God.[154]

Summary of the Main Points in 2 Thessalonians

The author of 2 Thessalonians writes to assure the Thessalonians that the Day of the Lord has not yet come. Those community members who have set aside work and are free-loading on the other members are to resume their work. There are certain conditions that will be evident when the Second Coming is to occur. In the meantime, the church is to live in readiness for the Lord's coming.

FOR FURTHER READING

Giblin, Charles Homer. "The Second Letter to the Thessalonians," in *The New Jerome Biblical Commentary.* Raymond E. Brown et al, eds. Englewood Cliffs, NJ: Prentice Hall, 1990, pp. 871–75.

Marshall, I. Howard. *1 and 2 Thessalonians.* New Century Bible Commentary. Ronald E. Clements et al, gen. eds. Grand Rapids, MI: Wm. B. Eerdmans Publishing Co., 1983.

Richard, Earl J. *First and Second Thessalonians.* Sacra Pagina Series #11. Daniel J. Harrington, S.J., ed. Collegeville, MN: The Liturgical Press, 1995.

Notes

1. Collins, Raymond F. "The First Letter to the Thessalonians" in *The New Jerome Biblical Commentary*. Raymond E. Brown et al., eds. Englewood Cliffs, NJ: Prentice Hall, 1990, p. 772.

2. *New Saint Joseph People's Prayer Book*. Rev. Francis Evans, gen. ed. New York: Catholic Book Publishing Co., 1980, # 729.

3. Collins, Raymond F. "1 Thessalonians," in *The New Jerome Biblical Commentary*, p. 778.

4. Collins, Raymond F. "The First Letter to the Thessalonians," *The New Jerome Biblical Commentary*, p. 778.

5. Grundmann, W. *"syn–meta"* in *Theological Dictionary of the New Testament*, Abridged One Volume, by Geoffrey W. Bromiley. Gerhard Kittel and Gerhard Friedrich, eds. Grand Rapids, MI: Eerdmans, 1985, pp. 1102–07.

6. *New Saint Joseph People's Prayer Book*, # 963.

7. Bertram, G. *"odin,* in *Theological Dictionary of the New Testament,* Abridged One Volume, by Geoffrey W. Bromiley, pp. 1353–54.

8. John Henry Newman. *Prayers, Poems, Meditations.* Selected and Introduced by A. N. Wilson. New York: Crossroads, 1990, p. 187.

9. Brown, Raymond E. *An Introduction to the New Testament.* New York: Doubleday, 1997, pp. 511–15.

10. Murphy-O'Connor, O.P., Jerome. "The First Letter to the Corinthians," in *The New Jerome Biblical Commentary*. Raymond E. Brown et al., eds. Englewood Cliffs, NJ: Prentice Hall, 1990, pp. 798–99.

11. Two or more of these letters are believed to be put together in 2 Corinthians.

12. *New Saint Joseph People's Prayer Book*, # 451.

13. Brown, Raymond E. *An Introduction to the New Testament*, p. 517.

14. *New Saint Joseph People's Prayer Book*, # 755.

15. Because there are no quotation marks in Greek, almost certainly this is a statement that came to Paul from the Corinthians and one to which Paul responds in the following sentences.

16. Collins, Raymond F. *First Corinthians*. Sacra Pagina Series, #VII, p. 258.

17. *New Saint Joseph People's Prayer Book*, # 577.

18. Dunn, James D. G. 1 *Corinthians*. New Testament Guides Series. Sheffield, England: Sheffield Academic Press, 1995, p. 78.

19. *New Saint Joseph People's Prayer Book*, # 374.

20. *Theological Dictionary of the New Testament*, p. 7.

21. *New Saint Joseph People's Prayer Book*, # 435.

22. Murphy-O'Connor,O.P., Jerome, "The First Letter to the Corinthians," in *The New Jerome Biblical Commentary*, p. 813.

23. Murphy-O'Connor, O.P., Jerome. "The First Letter to the Corinthians," in *The New Jerome Biblical Commentary*, p. 813.

24. Philo, a contemporary of Paul, was a Jewish philosopher.

25. Murphy-O'Connor, O.P., Jerome. "The First Letter to the Corinthians," in *The New Jerome Biblical Commentary*, pp. 813–14.

26. Cerfaux, Lucien. *The Spiritual Journey of St. Paul*. New York: Sheed and Ward, 1968, pp. 86–87.

27. Murphy-O'Connor, O.P., Jerome. "The First Letter to the Corinthians," in *The New Jerome Biblical Commentary*, p. 813.

28. *New Saint Joseph People's Prayer Book*, # 467.

29. Murphy-O'Connor, O.P., Jerome. "The Second Letter to the Corinthians," in *The New Jerome Biblical Commentary*, pp. 816–17.

30. The "Judaizers" were a group of Jewish Christians from Jerusalem who were insisting that the Gentiles observe the Jewish laws regarding circumcision and some other rituals.

31. Martin, Ralph. *2 Corinthians*, Word Biblical Commentary, vol. 40. Waco, TX: Word Books, 1986, pp. 9–10.

32. Thrall, Margaret E. *The Second Epistle to the Corinthians*. The International Critical Commentary. J. A. Emerton, C. E. B. Cranfield and G. E. Stanton, eds. Edinburgh, Scotland: T & T Clark, 1994, p. 610.

33. Greeven, H. *"deomai; deesis, prosdeomai,"* p. 144, and *"euchomai; euche; proseuchomai; proseuche,"* p. 279 in Gerhard Kittel's abridged volume of *Theological Dictionary of the New Testament*.

34. Best, Ernest. *Second Corinthians*. Interpretation Series. Atlanta: John Knox Press, 1987, p. 22.

35. *New Saint Joseph People's Prayer Book*. From "Communal Prayer Services for Ordinary Time," # 715.

36. *New Saint Joseph People's Prayer Book*, # 458.

37. *New Saint Joseph People's Prayer Book*, # 515.

38. Best, Ernest. *Second Corinthians*, p. 46.

39. See Thrall, Margaret E. *The Second Epistle to the Corinthians*, pp. 370–73.

40. Murphy-O'Connor, O.P., Jerome "The Second Letter to the Corinthians," in *The New Jerome Biblical Commentary*, p. 823.

41. Matera, Frank. *Galatians.* Sacra Pagina Series. Daniel Hallington, S.J., ed., vol. 9. Collegeville, MN: The Liturgical Press, 1992, pp. 83–84.

42. Best, Ernest. *Second Corinthians.* p. 77.

43. Prayer to St. Vincent de Paul from the *Liturgy of the Hours* for the feast of St. Vincent de Paul.

44. *Liturgy of the Hours;* Vol. I. New York: Catholic Book Pub., 1975, p. 1425.

45. Murphy-O'Connor, O.P., Jerome. "2 Corinthians," in *The New Jerome Biblical Commentary,* p. 828. Also St. John Chrysostom *Homilies 26.*

46. Barnett, Paul. *The Second Epistle to the Corinthians.* Grand Rapids, MI: William B. Eerdmans Publishing Co., 1997, p. 577.

47. *New Saint Joseph People's Prayer Book,* # 476.

48. Best, Ernest. *Second Corinthians,* pp. 124–25.

49. Martin, Ralph. *2 Corinthians,* p. 478.

50. *New Saint Joseph People's Prayer Book,* # 1210.

51. *New Saint Joseph People's Prayer Book,* #431.

52. Fitzmyer, S.J., Joseph A. "The Letter to Philemon" in *The New Jerome Biblical Commentary,* p. 871.

53. *New Saint Joseph People's Prayer Book,* # 772.

54. Fitzmyer, S.J., Joseph A. "The Letter to the Galatians," in *The New Jerome Biblical Commentary,* p. 780.

55. *New Saint Joseph People's Prayer Book,* # 443.

56. *New Saint Joseph People's Prayer Book,* # 486.

57. George, Timothy. *Galatians,* The New American Commentary Series, vol. 30. Nashville: Broadman and Holman Publishers, 1994.

58. Matera, Frank. *Galatians,* p. 115.

59. A rhetorical question is one to which a predetermined "yes" or "no" is expected.

60. Matera, Frank. *Galatians,* p. 123.

61. Fitzmyer, S.J., Joseph A. "The Letter to the Galatians," in *The New Jerome Biblical Commentary,* p. 781.

62. Matera, Frank. *Galatians,* p. 116.

63. EWTN http://ewtn.com/whatsnew.htm.

64. Matera, Frank. *Galatians,* p. 189.

65. *New Saint Joseph People's Prayer Book,* # 362.

66. Brown, Raymond E. *An Introduction to the New Testament,* p. 483.

67. Conzelmann, H. *"chairo, chara, synchairo,"* *TDNT,* abr. vol., p. 1300.

68. Hawthorne, Gerald F. *Philippians.* Word Biblical Commentary. Waco, TX: Word Books, 1983, p. 18.

69. Pope John Paul II. *Redemptoria Missio (Mission of the Redeemer).* Encyclical Letter, Dec. 7, 1990, # 71.

70. *New Saint Joseph People's Prayer Book,* # 507.

71. Hawthorne, Gerald F. *Philippians,* pp. 38–39.

72. Fee, Gordon D. *Paul's Letter to the Philippians,* p. 227.

73. Source unknown.

74. Hawthorne, Gerald F. *Philippians,* p. 170.

75. Hawthorne, Gerald F. *Philippians,* pp. 170–71.

76. Byrne, Brendan. "The Letter to the Philippians," in *The New Jerome Biblical Commentary,* Raymond E. Brown et al., eds. New York: Prentice Hall, 1990, p. 794.

77. *New Saint Joseph People's Prayer Book,* # 404.

78. For reference to this idea and much of the following, refer to Fitzmyer, S.J., Joseph A. *Romans.* Anchor Bible, vol. 33. New York: Doubleday, 1993, pp. 254ff.

79. Fitzmyer, Joseph A. *Romans,* pp. 264–65.

80. *New Saint Joseph People's Prayer Book,* # 439.

81. Fitzmyer, S.J., Joseph A. *Spiritual Exercises Based on Paul's Epistle to the Romans.* Mahwah, NJ: Paulist Press, 1995, p. 79.

82. LXX refers to the Septuagint, a second-century B.C. Greek translation of the Old Testament.

83. Fitzmyer, S.J., Joseph A. *Romans,* p. 348.

84. Fitzmyer, S.J., Joseph A. *Romans,* p. 350.

85. Fitzmyer, S.J., Joseph A. *Spiritual Exercises Based on Paul's Epistle to the Romans,* p. 59.

86. Byrne, S.J., Brendan. *Romans.* Sacra Pagina Series, Collegeville, MN: The Liturgical Press, 1996, p. 127.

87. Byrne, S.J., Brendan. *Romans.* Sacra Pagina Series, p. 142.

88. See Dicharry, Warren. *To Live the Word, Inspired and Incarnate.* New York: Alba House, 1985, p. 266.

89. Fitzmyer, S.J., Joseph A. *Romans,* p. 395.

90. Fitzmyer, S.J., Joseph A. *Spiritual Exercises Based on Paul's Epistle to the Romans,* p. 79.

91. Fitzmyer, S.J., Joseph A. *Romans,* p. 399.

92. Ulanov, Barry. *Prayers of St. Augustine.* Minneapolis, MN: The Seabury Press, 1983, pp. 68–69.

93. Mounce, Robert H. *NAC* 27. Nashville: Broadman & Holman Publishers, 1995, p. 149.

94. La Sor, William Sanford. "Discovering What Jewish *Miqva'ot* Can Tell Us About Christian Baptism," *Biblical Archaeology Review,* vol. VIII, no. 1, January/February, 1987, pp. 52–59.

95. Fitzmyer, S.J., Joseph A. *Spiritual Exercises Based on Paul's Epistle to the Romans,* p. 93.

96. Fitzmyer, S.J., Joseph A. *Spiritual Exercises Based on Paul's Epistle to the Romans,* pp. 95–96.

97.   Fitzmyer, S.J., Joseph A. *Spiritual Exercises Based on Paul's Epistle to the Romans*, p. 96.

98.   See Dicharry, Warren. *To Live the Word, Inspired and Incarnate*, p. 349.

99.   Byrne, S.J., Brendan. *Romans*, p. 240.

100. Byrne, S.J., Brendan. *Romans*, p. 239.

101. *New Saint Joseph People's Prayer Book*, # 500.

102. Byrne, S. J., Brendan. *Romans*, p. 282.

103. Fitzmyer, S. J., Joseph A. *Romans*, pp. 543–44.

104. Fitzmyer, S.J., Joseph A. *Romans*, p. 545.

105. Fitzmyer, S.J., Joseph A. *Spiritual Exercises Based on Paul's Epistle to the Romans*, p. 158.

106. Fitzmyer, S.J., Joseph A. *Romans*, pp. 559–60.

107. Fitzmyer, S.J., Joseph A. *Spiritual Exercises Based on Paul's Epistle to the Romans*, p. 161.

108. Byrne, S.J., Brendan. *Romans*, p. 310.

109. Fitzmyer, S.J., Joseph A. *Spiritual Exercises Based on Paul's Epistle to the Romans*, p. 165.

110. Bryne, S.J., Brendan. *Romans*, p. 340. Fitzmyer, S.J., Joseph A. *Romans*, pp. 613–14.

111. Fitzmyer, S.J., Joseph A. *Romans*, pp. 582–83.

112. EWTN: *http://www.ewtn.com.* SJS Home Page, 1.

113. Horgan, Maurya P. "The Letter to the Colossians," in *The New Jerome Biblical Commentary*, p. 876.

114. Dunn, James D. G. *The Epistles to the Colossians and to Philemon: A Commentary on the Greek Text.* Grand Rapids, MI: Eerdmans, 1996, p. 269. Brown, Raymond E. *An Introduction to the New Testament*, p. 614.

115. MacDonald, Margaret Y. *Colossians and Ephesians.* Sacra Pagina Series #17. Collegeville, MN: The Liturgical Press, 2000.

116. "Christology" deals with the identity of Christ as both human and divine.

117. Horgan, Maurya P., "The Letter to the Colossians," in *The New Jerome Biblical Commentary*, p. 55.

118. MacDonald, Margaret Y. *Colossians and Ephesians*, p. 11.

119. MacDonald, Margaret Y. *Colossians and Ephesians*, p. 44.

120. O'Brien, Peter T. *Colossians, Philemon.* Word Biblical Commentary # 44. Waco, TX: Word Books, 1982, p. 10.

121. O'Brien, Peter T. *Colossians, Philemon,* p. 11.

122. Stanley, S.J., David M. *Boasting in the Lord. The Phenomenon of Prayer in Saint Paul.* New York: Paulist Press, 1973, p. 157.

123. Prayers from the National Shrine of Saint Elizabeth Ann Seton. URL: http://www.webdesk.com/catholic/places/setonshrine/.

124. Karris, O.F.M., Robert J. *A Symphony of New Testament Hymns.* Collegeville, MN: The Liturgical Press, 1996.

125. Stanley, S.J., David M. *Boasting in the Lord,* p. 154.

126. Kittel, G., *"eikon"* in *Theological Dictionary of the New Testament,* Abridged One Volume, by G. Bromiley. Gerhard Kittel and Gerhard Friedrich, eds. Grand Rapids, MI: Eerdmans, 1985, pp. 203–6.

127. MacDonald, Margaret Y. *Colossians and Ephesians*, p. 59.

128. *The Oxford Book of Prayer.* George Appleton, gen. ed. Oxford: Oxford University Press, 1985, # 610.

129. To be firmly rooted or fixed as on a firm foundation.

130. *New Saint Joseph People's Prayer Book, # 408.*

131. Brown, Raymond E. *An Introduction to the New Testament,* p. 620.

132. Johnson, Luke T. *The Writings of the New Testament.* Philadelphia, PA: Fortress Press, 1986, pp. 367f.

133. MacDonald, Margaret Y. *Colossians and Ephesians*, p. 193.

134. "Eschatology" refers to the doctrine of the last things, such as the end of the world, judgment, and the inauguration of the kingdom of God in its finality.

135. "Deutero-Pauline" refers to letters written after the death of Paul. They maintain the apostle's theology and were probably written in the name of Paul to substantiate that fact.

136. Brown, Raymond E. *An Introduction to the New Testament,* p. 620.

137. Cerfaux, Lucien, *The Spiritual Journey of Saint Paul,* p. 155.

138. Taken from: *The Liturgy of the Hours.* Common of the Dedication of a Church. Evening Prayer II, Vol. IV, p. 1619.

139. Best, Ernest. *Ephesians.* New Testament Guides. A. T. Lincoln, ed. Sheffield: JSOT Press, 1993, p. 55.

140. Brown, Raymond E. *An Introduction to the New Testament,* p. 636.

141. See the discussion on household codes by MacDonald, Margaret Y. *Colossians and Ephesisans.* pp. 162–64.

142. See MacDonald, Margaret Y. *Colossians and Ephesians,* pp. 325–26 for possibility of this verse being connected to Eph 5:22.

143. Kobelski, Paul J., "The Letter to the Ephesians," in *The New Jerome Biblical Commentary,* p. 890.

144. *The Oxford Book of Prayer,* # 374.

145. Richard, Earl J. *First and Second Thessalonians.* Sacra Pagina Series # 11. Daniel J. Harrington, S.J., ed. Collegeville, MN: The Liturgical Press, 1995, pp. 19–24.

146. Brown, Raymond E. *An Introduction to the New Testament,* pp. 593–94.

147. Richard, Earl J. *First and Second Thessalonians,* pp. 301–5.

148. Giblin, Charles Homer. "The Second Letter to the Thessalonians," in *The New Jerome Biblical Commentary,* p. 873.

149. John Henry Newman: *Prayers, Poems, Meditations,* p. 147.

150. See Giblin, S. J., Charles Homer, "The Second Letter to the Thessalonians," in *The New Jerome Biblical Commentary,* p.873.

151. Giblin, S.J.,Charles Homer. "The Second Letter to the Thessalonians," pp. 871–72.

152. The difficulty of interpreting this passage and the many attempts at doing so are reflected in: F. F. Bruce, *1 & 2 Thessalonians,* Word Biblical Commentaries. Waco,TX: Word Books, 1982, pp. 163–88; also Bonnie Thurston, *Reading Colossians, Ephesians, & 2 Thessalonians.* New York: Crossroad, 1995, pp. 175–81.

153. See Brown, Raymond E. *An Introduction to the New Testament,* pp. 595–96.

154. *New Saint Joseph People's Prayer Book,* #410.